NOV 1 4 2006

Victoria

Wedding Cakes
and Flowers

D1361532

Victoria

Wedding Cakes and Flowers

Kathleen Hackett
Allison Kyle Leopold with Gerit Quealy

Hearst Books
A Division of Sterling Publishing Co., Inc.
New York

ROUND LAKE AREA
LIBRARY
906 HART ROAD
ROUND LAKE, IL 60073
(847) 546-7060

Copyright © 2006 by Hearst Communications, Inc.

This book was previously published in 2003 as two separate hardcover books:
Wedding Cakes and *Wedding Flowers*.

Book design by Alexander Isley Inc.

All rights reserved. The written instructions and photographs in this volume are intended
for the personal use of the reader and may be reproduced for that purpose only. Any other use, especially
commercial use, is forbidden under law without the written permission of the copyright holder.

Every effort has been made to ensure that all the information in this book is accurate. However, due to
differing conditions, tools, and individual skills, the publisher cannot be responsible for any injuries, loss-
es, and/or other damages that may result from the use
of the information in this book.

Library of Congress Cataloging-in-Publication Data
Hackett, Kathleen.
  Victoria : wedding cakes and flowers / Kathleen Hackett, Allison Kyle Leopold,
with Gerit Quealy.
      p. cm.
  Includes bibliographical references and index.
  ISBN-13: 978-1-58816-615-9
  ISBN-10: 1-58816-615-5
  1. Wedding cakes. 2. Wedding decorations. 3. Flower arrangement. 4. Bridal bouquets. I. Leopold,
Allison Kyle. II. Quealy, Gerit. III. Title.
  TX771.H2176 2006
  745.92'6--dc22

                            2006008275

10 9 8 7 6 5 4 3 2 1

Published by Hearst Books
A Division of Sterling Publishing Co., Inc.
387 Park Avenue South, New York, NY 10016

Hearst Books is proud to continue the superb style, quality, and tradition of *Victoria* magazine
with every book we publish. On our beautifully illustrated pages you will always find inspiration and ideas
about the subjects you love.

Victoria and Hearst Books are trademarks of Hearst Communications, Inc.
Cool Whip is a registered trademark of Kraft Food.
Crisco is a registered trademark of J.M. Smucker Company.

For information about custom editions, special sales, premium and
corporate purchases, please contact Sterling Special Sales Department at
800-805-5489 or specialsales@sterlingpub.com.

Distributed in Canada by Sterling Publishing
c/o Canadian Manda Group, 165 Dufferin Street
Toronto, Ontario, Canada M6K 3H6

Distributed in Australia by Capricorn Link (Australia) Pty. Ltd.
P.O. Box 704, Windsor, NSW 2756 Australia

Manufactured in China

Sterling ISBN 13: 978-1-58816-615-9
      ISBN 10: 1-58816-615-5

Page 2: *Even if you're planning on wearing a veil, you can still wear flowers on your head. Keep them simple, though, so as not to overwhelm the veil. Here, a single, perfect hydrangea anchors a delicate veil to the bride's hair.*

Contents

Part I
Wedding Cakes

In all of the wedding cake,
hope is the sweetest of plums.

—Douglas Jerrold

Introduction

Wedding cakes are as magical as romance and as varied as brides and grooms. Today the classic tiered white wedding cake is only one of the many styles a couple can choose from. The sweetest symbol of a couple's new life together, a wedding cake can be a towering stack of tiers separated by columns and bursting with flowers, a charming layer cake swathed in swirls of seven-minute frosting, an architectural wonder with crisp edges covered in fondant or even a tower of cupcakes. The cake can also be more personal. There are hundreds of ways to tastefully incorporate favorite flowers, a beloved lace pattern, and the details of a wedding dress onto a wedding cake.

These pages are designed to inspire you to consider the unlimited possibilities for your wedding cake, both on the outside and inside. There is almost nothing a talented baker can't do, as you will see on the pages that follow. If the fresh flowers you love are out of season, have them rendered in buttercream instead. If your favorite color is woven throughout your ceremony and reception, then ask your baker if a tinted cake would be possible. If you and your groom are nature lovers, discuss the possibilities for conveying the mountains or woodlands or seashore that you love on your cake. Carrot, lemon, chocolate or spice, whatever flavor you fancy, can surely become part of your wedding cake choice. Drape the layers in royal icing, buttercream, fondant, Swiss meringue, chocolate or *seven-minute* frosting, whichever is your favorite.

Whether you are celebrating in front of the fire in your living room or in the grand ballroom of a hotel, you will find these pages brimming with ideas and essential information for creating the cake of your dreams.

Page 6: *A charming, single-tiered cake covered in drifts of coconut needs only a homespun tablecloth and a simple glass cake stand to look stylish.*

Opposite: *A classic white cake covered in fondant and draped with pearls of royal icing is always elegant. The tightly bound topper of pink roses adds a romantic blush of color.*

CHAPTER I

The Dream

Something old, something new, something borrowed, something blue . . . For generations, tradition has allowed the bride to choose her wedding dress as well as mementos and keepsakes to create her own very personal vision of something old, new, borrowed, and blue. However, when it came to the wedding cake there was no latitude for choice. Traditionally, it had to be a three-tiered white-frosted cake with a plastic or porcelain bride and groom perched on top.

Times have changed. Modern wedding cakes are far more reflective of a couple's shared personal style. In fact, there are probably as many different weddings cakes as there are brides and grooms. For many couples, the wedding cake makes a vivid style statement—as important as the wedding dress and the venue they choose to marry in. If you think back to the last three or four weddings you attended, chances are that each cake was vastly different from the other—and one was probably saturated in color! As a bride-to-be you will find hundreds of wedding cake styles, colors, and flavors to choose from, and the traditional white tiered cake is just one of them.

Page 10: *A swath of roses skims across a three-tiered white cake, dressing it up for the occasion. An experienced baker can create almost any flower desired in frosting.*

Right: *Your wedding cake can be anything you want it to be, so long as it reflects your personal style. For one couple with a shared passion for flower gardening, a tower of cupcakes in full bloom struck the perfect note at their casual outdoor reception.*

Opposite: *Two dozen yellow rosebuds carpet the top of this festive, two-tiered cake, perfectly suited for a small restaurant wedding. Lush cornflower satin ribbon delineates the tiers and adds a colorful note to what began as a traditional white cake.*

The "something blue" at a wedding today could well be the cake.

Your wedding reception is likely to be the most elaborate party you will ever give and your wedding cake the most memorable dessert you will ever serve. Displayed at the reception with the same reverence as a beloved work of art, your wedding cake should be given as much consideration as every other major decision you make about your big day. How your cake looks is of utmost importance, but how it tastes is an equally important reflection of your personal style and unique sensibility.

Whether your taste runs toward the traditional or the modern, the style of your wedding cake is only as limited as your imagination and the mood you want to create at your big party. If you want a teetering tower of layer cakes bursting with gum-paste flowers on every surface, tell your cake designer and discuss how to make your dream a reality. If you've always envisioned a three-tiered, white-frosted cake with a traditional topper, then that is what you should have. But if a rich chocolate layer cake with chocolate buttercream frosting bedecked in deep red roses reflects your passion, then don't hesitate to put that on display for all your guests to marvel at.

In Victorian England, a wedding cake was considered fit for the occasion only if it consisted of three white tiers set on columns, decorated in white, and embellished with piped sugar frosting.

There are a few decisions, however, that are best made before you choose what kind of wedding cake you will have. Determine the date, location, and number of guests attending your wedding before you begin to fantasize about the cake of your dreams. Once you have made these decisions, your wedding will begin to have a specific feeling, mood, or theme, which should be echoed in the style of your cake. The season of your wedding, the size of the cake needed, and the accessibility of the wedding site can also influence your choice of flavors, ingredients, and decoration. Once you have confirmed the logistical details, you can begin to talk to a baker and seek out inspiration for a cake that is uniquely yours.

Right and opposite: *Your cake doesn't have to be formal. A casual summer wedding at the beach inspired this sweet seashell confection.*

Inspiration is All Around You

There are hundreds of places to seek inspiration for your wedding cake style, many of them closer than you might think. Of course, magazines and books are sure to spark your creativity, but to achieve a truly individual—and memorable—sweet ending to your blissful day, just look around you.

Your dress is an excellent, and many bakers will tell you, the only source of inspiration needed to make a glorious wedding cake. Most cake bakers will ask you to bring your dress to them so that they can see the color, texture, and stylistic details up close. The color can easily be translated to the icing if you're after an elegant, monochromatic theme. What's more, buttons, bows, ruffles, and pleats can all be re-created on a cake to mimic the style of your dress. If your dress is covered in passementerie, that too can be rendered on the tiers of the cake in buttercream or gum-paste scrolls.

In addition, it helps before visiting your baker to put together a mini scrapbook of words, pictures, swatches, and any other items that will help convey your vision for your wedding cake.

Opposite: A four-tiered, all white cake can be both grand and understated at the same time. This confection is simply adorned with only slender swags looping along each tier, a bouquet of gum-paste roses on top, and a ring of gardenias for table decoration.

Left, top: A crown of fresh garden roses in varying shades of pink rings a single tier, the perfect cake for a small, elegant summer reception at home.

Left, bottom: Inspired by a set of beloved family china passed from one generation to the next, one bride honored tradition by having the nostalgic pattern translated onto her cake.

Include that piece of lace you have been saving just because you love it. And don't hesitate to add the paint chip with the color you painted your favorite room. And what about a swatch of that dotted Swiss dress your mother surprised you with on your tenth birthday?

Most patterns, colors, and textures can be re-created on your cake by an expert cake baker. Could the sweet floral pattern on the cherished handkerchief from your grandmother provide the decoration inspiration for a beautiful and poignant cake?

The **seasons** are also wonderful sources of **inspiration**, particularly if you are marrying on or near a **holiday**.

Can you picture the family china that has been passed on to you translated into beautifully colored swirls of frosting?

Consider the location of your wedding as a source of inspiration, too. A woodland setting may suggest a cake draped in elegant buttercream greenery depicting ferns or hostas. If your party is under a tent in an open field of wildflowers, by all means, consider incorporating them into your cake. If you are having an elaborate celebration in a fancy hotel ballroom, look closely at the décor and architecture of the room; there may be shapes and colors that are beautifully suited to the structure and decoration of your cake.

The seasons are also wonderful sources of inspiration, particularly if you are marrying on or near a holiday. Are you planning a spring wedding in Vermont? What could be more charming and delicious than a maple sugar layer cake to evoke the state's most delicious delicacy? Are you getting married in the Pacific Northwest this summer, when huckleberries are at their peak? Nothing makes a cake look more enticing than fresh, abundant regional fruit. A Christmas wedding cake can be as ethereal as a snowy coconut layer cake or as over-the-top as a lavishly decorated tree-shaped cake iced in chocolate and sprinkled with powdered sugar to imitate fallen snow.

Opposite: A wedding cake can be a poignant reference to your ancestry. This traditional Scandinavian wedding cake—a towering pyramid of marzipan rings, each drizzled with white royal icing—is as breathtaking as any wedding cake can be.

THE DREAM

If your family history and traditions have played a strong role in your life, perhaps you should look to your heritage for clues to creating a memorable wedding cake. If you hail from a strong French lineage—or maybe you first vacationed with your betrothed in Paris—you may consider forgoing a traditional layer cake and do as the French do: Celebrate the occasion with a **croquembouche**, an elaborate dessert made with caramel-coated custard-filled cream puffs stacked into a tall pyramid and draped in spun sugar. A bride of Scandinavian descent might choose the Danish marzipan ring cake, the customary wedding cake in Denmark. A masterpiece of almonds, pastillage, and marzipan, this cake is filled with fresh fruit, candy, and almond cakes.

If you love the idea of acknowledging your heritage but don't care for the wedding cakes found in your ancestral country, consider creating a cake from other traditional sweets and confections. The wonderful and colorful variety of Italian cookies available in good Italian bakeries make clever and delicious

"cakes" when artfully stacked in tiers. And why not honor your Mexican bloodlines by sculpting a pyramid of Mexican wedding cakes, the powdered sugar-covered shortbread cookies so popular during the holidays. Don't hesitate to mention your favorite sweet or dessert to your baker, no matter how irrelevant it may seem. It may spark an idea that you thought impossible to create.

Ideas can come from seemingly unlikely places; even scenes from still-life paintings are rich resources, if not for the specific cake and its decorations then certainly for the mood they can inspire you to create. Chardin, Vermeer, Manet, Monet, Degas, Van Gogh, and more contemporary artists such as Wayne Thiebaud render shapes, colors, and emotions that may be exactly what you want to convey with your cake. Chardin's "The Buffet" for example, features a towering pyramid of fresh fruit made from an assemblage of several compotes arranged at varying heights—a concept you may be able to re-create with an assemblage of cakes. You could also look at paintings and ceramics in your local museums or in art books at your local library or bookstore.

Movies, too, can spark moods and visual ideas that can be extended to your wedding cake. The French movie **Chocolat** may inspire an all-chocolate extravaganza, while **Babette's Feast** could convince you that a buffet reception with a fabulous cake as the centerpiece suits your style perfectly. Pick up videos and look at **The Wedding Banquet**, **Like Water for Chocolate**, **Eat Drink Man Woman**, and **Chef in Love**. All movies centered on food and feasting, they are sure to awaken your creativity,

And don't feel you have to arrive at your baker's with dozens of ideas. If you are the kind of bride who knows exactly what you want, the items in your scrapbook may be limited to one or two entries. If you can't imagine a cake without your favorite flower, berry, or tree incorporated into the cake, then that's all you need to show your baker.

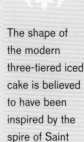

The shape of the modern three-tiered iced cake is believed to have been inspired by the spire of Saint Bride's Church in the City of London.

Opposite: *A classic white cake can be used as a canvas for all manner of decoration. A cornucopia of vibrant roses tumbling down the tiers gives this otherwise quiet white confection flamboyance and style.*

CHAPTER 2

Sweet Possibilities

Classic White Cakes

It is the color of purity and a symbol of innocence. When white is baked into the layers of a wedding cake and spun into icing that graces each tier in loopy swirls, exacting patterns, or in a smooth gleaming coat, only the bride herself can compare to its breathtaking beauty. White weddings are as timeless as matrimony itself, and a classic white wedding cake will only emphasize a couple's reverence for the rituals of love and marriage.

White wedding cakes first appeared in Victorian times, when only affluent families were able to obtain the finest refined sugars for making icing. In those days, the more refined and expensive the sugar, the whiter the cake. No longer an indication of affluence, a classic white wedding cake remains among the most popular with bridal couples, both for celebrating the strong traditions associated with a wedding day as well as for evoking endless visions of individual style.

Time was when all white wedding cakes looked and tasted essentially the same. Traditionally, three tiers were separated by columns and draped with white royal icing. Today, a white wedding cake can take on many shapes, styles, and even

flavors, depending on the personal style of the bridal couple. Cakes can range in presentation from fanciful and playful to stately and majestic, and in flavors as delicate as orange blossom or vanilla bean to more assertive versions such as toasted almond or white chocolate.

The only rules a couple need follow are the obvious: To qualify as classic a white wedding cake must be white inside and out and arranged in tiers, on columns or stacked. The shape may be square, round, oval, hexagonal, or petal. In addition to the traditional royal icing, the tiers can be frosted in fondant, Swiss meringue buttercream, white chocolate ganache, and seven-minute frosting.

Page 22: Something blue? A classic white cake swathed in butter-cream and bursting with roses is beautifully embellished with an eggshell-blue ribbon.

Opposite: The smooth tiers of a white wedding cake are set on dowels to give this cake height. Tiny rosebuds tightly tucked in between provide both beautiful and textural layers to the cake and hide the framework that holds it steady. The piped butter-cream ruffles make the confection flow seamlessly from cake layer to rosebuds.

This page: The classic five-tiered white cake is always visually stunning. The flowers chosen for your bouquet can also provide the perfect finishing touch for your cake.

Page 26: Single strands of gleaming silver dragées are exquisite when used sparingly, as they are in this refined white fondant-covered cake. Gum-paste roses spill modestly across the tiers without compromising its manicured look, while a silk bow topper adds a whimsical air.

All are beautiful and delicious, but each one has special attributes, which may make it more or less ideal for the effect you want to create. Royal icing was at one time the only frosting considered appropriate for white wedding cakes. Today it is used to evoke even more elaborate and decorative effect than in Victorian times. It is a wonderful medium for creating piped decorations, which can be fashioned into bows and swags to swing around a cake, or into decorative borders to give the cake a finished look. It is also the perfect medium for gluing decorations to the cake.

Swiss meringue buttercream can be applied in broad strokes for an informal, whimsical look, or it can be piped through all manner of tips to create lush, yet precise, traditional patterns such as wickerwork and ruffles or designs that echo the details of the bride's white dress. In fact, Swiss meringue buttercream is so versatile that it can be used to render elements of the wedding setting right onto the cake. For example, if your celebration is in a clapboard cottage by the sea, the clapboard pattern can be piped right onto the cake. If you have your heart set

Page 27: Sugar dough ribbons and flowers come to life when arranged as if tumbling down the smooth tiers of a classic white wedding cake.

Right, top: Nature seems to produce flowers in every color imaginable—even those on your favorite china pattern. Study the colors you want to duplicate and then determine which flowers best mimic them. Choose those that are appropriately sized for your cake, and be sure that they will stay fresh through the reception.

Right, bottom: If special occasions always mean pulling out the family china, then what better celebration than a wedding—and more delicious medium than a wedding cake—to recall the pattern? Cascades of fresh flowers and bands of grosgrain ribbon adorn this traditional white cake, bringing a treasured china pattern to life.

on a pure white cake, however, keep in mind that butter-cream—made with butter—is actually the color of ivory.

If you're after a formal, tailored look, consider fondant, a pliable sugar dough that can be rolled out and draped onto the tiers of a cake for a satiny smooth finish. Fondant not only provides an incomparably smooth surface on which to arrange cake decorations but can be used as a canvas for making impressions, from quilted patterns made with a dressmaker's wheel to repeated borders made by pressing a piping tip into the fondant itself.

A classic white wedding cake is best compared to the little black dress: It is always fitting, unerringly timeless, and always looks good. You can dress it up or down (buttercream, royal icing, or fondant?), depending on the mood and tone you want to set. White embellishments—fresh, crystallized, or gum-paste flowers; royal icing or gum-paste ruffles, lace, swirls, swags, buttons, bows, petals, leaves, shells, dots, and zigzags—can bedeck the tiers. And with the variety of flavorings and fillings available now, it is sure to taste fabulous.

Left, top: *Expert cake artists can translate almost any dream of a cake into a reality. For one bride, an elaborately decorated porcelain box just had to inform her wedding cake design. Three tiers are stacked one atop the other, covered in tinted fondant, and bedecked with royal icing. A fourth tier is an exact replica of the box and the perfect place to tuck a tiny posy of fresh flowers.*

Left, bottom: *Bands of gold royal icing are remarkable imitations of the hinged and clasped box.*

Colorful Cakes

A wedding cake drenched in color is always a showstopper, particularly if it aptly reflects the personalities and styles of the bride and groom. For some couples, a colorful cake is deeply meaningful, in some cases a tribute to a beloved family member or heirloom. Great-grandmother's patterned handkerchief, the flamboyant family china, the 1940s wallpaper that still hangs in the summer cottage, mother's Fabergé jewel box—even the antique fabric from grandfather's favorite chair—can all be rendered in icing and decorations on your cake.

Because colorful cakes can be so magnificent, they are becoming more popular. Artist Wendy Kromer's Wedgwood cake echoes the patterns of the classic china. It is a masterpiece of blue-tinted fondant tiers decorated with creamy white designs and is a frequent choice with the clients of her wedding cake "boutique." A close second in popularity among her customers is her primrose cake, in which vividly colored flowers come to life against soft-toned icing to mimic the Tuscan Majolica earthenware that inspired it.

Whether you envision your wedding cake awash in color in both the icing and decorations, or displaying eye-popping decorations fixed against a classic white background, there are many ways to incorporate color into your wedding cake. If it is

Above: Blown sugar pearls of ivory and gold bob and weave along the tiers of a whimsical "painted" cake that is anything but conventional. A passion for impressionist art might inspire a cake such as this.

difficult to choose a single color, consider covering the layers in different tones of one hue or alternating two shades, such as pink and lavender. If a classic white cake **and** color are appealing, satisfy both desires by frosting the tiers in colored ribbons of marzipan or buttercream.

Of course, your cake can be any color you like, but consult your cake baker before you set your heart on a particular shade. While most cake professionals can achieve the impossible, experience has taught them that some icing and decoration materials take better to certain colors than others. If you want your cake to look as mouthwatering as it is awe-inspiring you may have to make minor adjustments to match both cake and frosting to your chosen color.

You might also take your color cues from the colors and flavors of the season. A spring wedding might inspire a cake mirroring the various shades of young spring greenery. An autumn wedding, on the other hand, lends itself beautifully to a cake covered in golden,

Page 31: The open weave of this royal iced cake creates just enough space to add tiny lavender designs, giving an overall impression that the cake is not white. A generous bundle of deeper-purple sweet peas reinforces the "color" of this otherwise simple white confection. All the while feather-weight butterflies made from royal icing flutter along the tiers.

Right: The cake stand can also add to the visual impact of a wedding cake. Here color is used only sparingly on the cake itself. Instead, it is concentrated in the cake stand, with small hints of hue appearing in fine bands and flowers on the cake's tiers.

red, orange, and yellow leaves rendered in marzipan, buttercream, or royal icing. Seasonal flavors can also dictate the colors of a cake. A winter wedding cake might feature the fruit colors of the season—citrus yellows, oranges, greens, and reds—or the warmer, richer tones of chocolate and nuts. A couple getting married on the seashore need only take a walk on the beach to find breezy color inspiration. The variously shaded blues and greens of sea glass; the corals, pinks, violets, and silvers of seashells; and the sky, water, sand, and grasses can all be echoed sweetly on a summer wedding cake.

The most obvious place to look for color inspiration is the flowers you will carry, the decorations you've chosen for the ceremony and the reception, and the colors you've chosen for the wedding party. Wherever you find the colors that best reflect your style, arrive at your meeting with your cake designer with the colorful swatches and objects that you hope to translate onto your cake. No amount of verbal description can replace seeing the real thing.

THEIR PIECE OF CAKE

No matter where couples live, they have two requirements when it comes to choosing a wedding cake: It must taste delicious and look beautiful, whether simple and elegant, or ornate and stately. Still, there are some regional preferences.

New York City—Square, stacked cakes with neoclassical designs are very popular.

New England—Flavor rules: Chocolate cake with chocolate ganache filling and icing is a favorite; so are lemon pound cake with raspberry filling and buttercream frosting, carrot cake with buttercream filling and frosting; chocolate cake with chocolate mousse filling.

Chicago/Midwest—Pillars are still favored here, and more and more couples are requesting square cakes. As for flavor, almond cake with custard filling and buttercream frosting is a top choice.

Dallas, Texas—The traditional tiered white cake with white filling and either white chocolate ganache or fondant frosting is the top pick. It is most often decorated with simple, elegant pastillage flowers.

Floral Cakes

Like love and marriage, flowers and wedding cakes are made for each other. And for every couple choosing a wedding cake, there is a sweet combination that is perfectly suited to them. Flowers can dance delicately around each tier, as if casually scattered like wildflowers, or they can spill from tier to tier in tight bunches, spiraling grandly from top to bottom. They can cover every surface of a cake for a painterly look or bloom here and there on a smooth backdrop for a more graphic presentation. For the minimalist couple, flowers can show up in just one place, in a smartly arranged bouquet on top of the cake. Flowers can bring your personal style to life, whether you want to present your sweet and delicate side or that gregarious and eccentric streak. Perhaps the least contrived of all cake decorations, fresh flowers are an incomparable choice if your tastes run toward the fresh and natural.

Just as the bridal bouquet and any floral decorations are chosen with the season, availability, and viability in mind, so too should flowers be selected. Chances are, the flowers you choose for the other elements of your wedding will be incorporated into

Opposite: An array of pastel blooms is all the decoration this simple white cake needs to look lovely. But make sure any flowers you choose are sturdy enough to stay fresh throughout the reception.

Page 36: Roses and primroses seem to grow naturally from the base tiers of this charming cake. Two hexagonal tiers separated by a perfectly round one give the flowers several varied surfaces upon which to bloom.

FRESH FLOWERS FOR YOUR CAKE—WHICH ONES WORK BEST

Once you've chosen the fresh flowers to adorn your cake—and determined that they are safe—you will want to be confident that they will thrive throughout the wedding reception until the cake is cut. Experienced cake designers will have expert suggestions on which flowers hold up well in specific weather conditions and for the duration of the wedding celebration. New England wedding cake baker Christine Deonis prefers working with "cluster" flowers, including delphiniums, lilacs, hydrangea, stock, or larkspur because they can be snipped off individually and scattered onto the cake. Unfussy flowers, such as orchids, calla lilies, tulips, gardenias, and daisies also work well. Edible flowers are always a charming adornment, and there are many to choose from that will work beautifully, including violets, pansies, roses, chrysanthemums, Johnny jump-ups, lilacs, and petunias.

your cake. Be sure that your florist and wedding cake designer are informed of your desires. Who is responsible for the flowers on the cake, the florist or the cake designer? Be sure to coordinate their efforts.

While the possibilities for fresh-flower choices seem infinite, there are some limitations when it comes to those that grace your wedding cake. Flowers essentially fall into three categories: edible, which means you can eat them safely; nontoxic, flowers that are safe to use for decoration but must be removed before the cake is served; and toxic, which should never come into contact with a wedding cake. If you have your heart set on beautiful yet toxic daffodils, wisteria, sweet peas, or irises, make sure you've chosen a baker who can render them in icing. Your florist and cake designer will be able to tell you which flowers are appropriate. If a generous friend or amateur cake baker is making the cake and wants to use fresh flowers, be sure to check their safety with a professional. All fresh flowers used for decorating a cake, whether edible or nontoxic, should be grown pesticide-free.

While fresh flowers are the easiest and least expensive way to achieve a beautiful cake, the seasonal and safety limitations are of no consequence if the blossoms are made from edible

Left and below: Nature lovers never want to be far from it and why should they? Butter-cream bees and butter-flies flit about the tiers of this colorful cake, their destination seeming to be the spray of silk flowers that adorns the top.

Below: *A few simple decorations can turn a traditional white cake into one that befits the season. Tiny crab apples, autumn leaves, and berries are arranged as if they had fallen from the trees onto the tiers of a buttercream-covered cake.*

CAKE WISE

"If I am working with fresh flowers, I prefer to work with rolled fondant. It is easier to remove the flowers from the cake before serving it. I also prefer to place a precut piece of clear plastic or cellophane on the top of the tier where the flowers may touch the cake. You don't see the plastic and the flowers won't be in direct contact with the icing. Always notify whoever will be cutting the cake to remove ALL flowers unless they are edible."—Wendy Kromer, boutique wedding cake designer, New York City

ingredients. Cover an entire cake with lilies of the valley in piped buttercream, or replicate a field of black-eyed Susans in gum paste. If your favorite roses are difficult

to come by, ask your cake designer to craft them from sugar. Many cake designers make beautiful crystallized versions of flowers, too.

Cakes Inspired by Nature

Did you meet while hiking the Appalachian Trail? Or taking a canoeing class? Is your cabin in the woods your favorite getaway? Does a field of wildflowers remind you of your first date? Did he propose on a walk through the woods? More than ever before, couples are requesting cakes that serve as symbols of a memorable moment, place, or experience in their relationship. Cakes covered with buttercream ferns, marzipan wild strawberries, Swiss meringue mushrooms, and gum-paste pinecones are as breathtaking as any, especially when they are tied to a romantic or poignant personal memory.

Cake designer Ron Ben-Israel once had a client request a cake dancing with buzzing marzipan bees on each tier. The bees were symbolic of the groom's commendable attempts to propose. In his first effort, he was down on his knee when a bee stung him, sending him to the hospital. In a repeat effort—this time indoors in the winter—another bee found him and stung him again. He succeeded on his third attempt. The tongue-in-cheek—and charming—reference to his perseverance, portrayed by the decorative bees on the wedding cake, forever etched in the couple's memories the moment of proposal.

Informal, Elegant Cakes

If you want your wedding day to exude a casual air, carry the mood right through to your cake. **Informal** does not mean "ordinary," and an unfussy cake is anything but when it is presented with elegance. Thoughtfully restraining the scale, size, and decorations on a wedding cake can create as much impact as a teetering tower of bedecked tiers. A simple cake can sport jaunty polka dots rendered in royal icing, as

Above: *Playful polka dots are piped in graphic columns and rows on this sweet cake, perfectly suited to an atmosphere that is both lighthearted and elegant.*

long as the accompanying decorations are scaled accordingly. Loopy swirls of seven-minute frosting are exquisite when they cover a small cake adorned only with shards of pure white coconut. A single-tiered, monochromatic cake decorated with a repeated piped pattern and set on a classic cake stand is handsome enough to star at a wedding luncheon or a small evening wedding.

If you want to create an informal mood, and even a low-tiered layer cake still seems too imposing, consider a sheet cake. Covered in fondant, a square sheet cake is as intriguing as grandmother's jewel box. And decorated with fresh or gum-paste flowers, it is perfect for a wedding tea or luncheon. Or you can create a casual cake composed of several tiers, as long as it is covered with broad strokes of icing or with a sleek coat of fondant and ganache and sparingly decorated.

One of the most popular ways to maintain an air of informality and still incorporate tiers is by arranging fancifully decorated cupcakes onto graduated sizes of cake stands, stacked to mimic the shape of a wedding cake. This playful choice allows guests several different flavors of cupcakes to choose from. Another plus, wedding cupcakes makes serving a breeze as there is no cake to cut—guests simply help themselves.

Opposite: Several small cakes have big impact when expertly decorated and presented. Variously shaped square and tall tiers plus a flamboyant topper give these cakes a personality all their own.

Above: A wedding tea calls for a delicate cake served on fine china. A square jewel-box of a confection, delicately decorated, is the perfect way to celebrate a simple ceremony at home.

CHAPTER 3

The Right Baker

Finding the right person to bake your wedding cake is as important as landing on a pair of wedding shoes that you can dance in all night. You need to find a good fit if you want to leave your wedding reception smiling. The best place to start is by asking friends whose wedding cakes you've remembered, both before and after they were cut. Most professional pastry chefs will leave their business cards with the reception staff or the bride; it is perfectly appropriate to ask for one if you like what you've seen and tasted.

Word of mouth can often turn up the best cake bakers. Perhaps your friend's friend works in the food business and can give you a list of proven bakers and pastry chefs, or your colleague's husband manages a banquet hall where hundreds of weddings are held each year. If a hotel or country club will be both hosting and catering the event, the staff wedding manager may strongly urge—or even require—that you use the in-house baker or one affiliated. The local telephone directory, bridal shops, bridal shows, and the Internet are all excellent places to begin your search.

A wedding planner, should you choose to work with one, can usually recommend a preferred baker or two. So, too, can most independent caterers or florists you interview. Be sure to see that person's portfolio and have a cake tasting before agreeing to use him or her. If you choose a different baker, inquire as to whether the venue adds an additional fee for cutting the cake. This is sometimes negotiable. Don't overlook your neighborhood bakery, even though they don't display wedding cakes in their window. They may make simple wedding cakes that are perfectly suited to your style.

You might even discover a gifted "cottage" baker with a passion for perfection, someone with experience who handles just a few special orders from home and does them beautifully. If your friend Annie or an enthusiastic relative who "loves making cakes" volunteers to make your wedding cake, a word of caution: It's not that a home-baked cake can't be delicious and pretty. But professional bakers have ovens, storage, and packing equipment as well as delivery and setup arrangements that help guarantee your cake arrives intact no matter the weather and survives intact to the grand moment of its cutting.

Regardless of the resources you use, make sure that you make appointments to meet the bakers three to six months in advance, especially if you plan to use a

Page 42: Don't be afraid of strong color—it can be both dramatic and beautiful. Here, roses in bold hues add visual impact to a gleaming white cake.

Right: Chocolate ganache shimmers on a handsome, three-tiered cake adorned with fresh fruit and flowers. Sugared champagne grapes, lemons, and beach plums are strewn among fresh cherries and roses in full bloom.

Opposite: An altogether different arrangement of fresh fruit and flowers accessorizes a formal white cake. Covered in fondant and bejeweled with royal icing pearl "necklaces," the elegant tiers need nothing more than a sugared lemon and a small bouquet of roses to give the stacks a finished look. Rose petals and fruit set the stage on which the cake sits.

popular cake designer, and if the person is a real star, a year ahead is occasionally required.

Since the early 1980s, when splendid wedding cakes by star bakers such as Sylvia Weinstock, Gail Watson, and Ron Ben-Israel became the breathtaking centerpieces of notable celebrations, more and more bakers throughout the country have studied and mastered the techniques of artistic decoration. Nowadays, you're far more likely to find such a person nearby than when your mom got married. Some skilled decorators offer just a few variations of flavors and fillings. But increasingly, brides are requesting, and getting, a cake that embodies the mouthwatering versatility of a true pâtissier.

Taste Before You Order

Some pastry chefs charge for consultations, while others factor it into the per/slice cost of the finished wedding cake. Ask what the policy is before you make the appointment and inquire, too, whether there will be samples to taste and pictures of previous work. If the baker hesitates to provide either of these, reconsider your choice. Though bakers with a bridal specialty can show you portfolios of their previous

Opposite: A lush butter-cream ruffle rings the top of a single-tiered cake set on a rimmed glass cake stand. Stephanotis, a classic wedding flower, and delicate purple blooms are just the right scale for this petite yet shapely cake.

Left: Why not add a touch of whimsy to your wedding? If a tree of chocolate gum-paste leaves is what you desire, then your cake baker can surely make it. On this fun-loving cake, individually wired leaves are tucked into the tree's "trunk" and set off-center on the top.

creations, and many today have websites as well, there's no substitute for a visit, a tasting, and a personal consultation. This is the time to discuss your ideas, consider new ones, and get an idea of the costs involved.

Remember that the more renowned the baker, the busier and the farther ahead you may need to lock in your dates. Have you finally landed on a date when your favorite inn on the lake is available? Alas, that doesn't mean the baker is also free that day. The busy season for weddings now stretches well beyond June and includes major holidays. In fact, early autumn, with its dazzling weather, is almost as popular a time for vows as early summer. So if you are enthusiastic about the baker, book your date. Most wedding cake designers prefer to meet couples after they have made most of the major wedding day decisions: date, time of day, venue, basic style. If all the lovely details—aside from the date—have not yet come together, you and the baker can always fine-tune the cake design later.

There are several questions, both practical and fanciful, that your baker will ask in order to help you create the cake of your wedding-day dreams. On the practical side, he or she will need to know such basic information as wedding date, place (indoors

Right: A multitiered "cake" can also be created in cupcakes. In this tower, 50 cupcakes are arranged in graduated tiers with a two-layer cake on top. Sunflowers and hydrangeas are rendered in buttercream, dressing the crest of each cupcake as well as the top tier.

Opposite: The simplest decorations can be the most showstopping. A simple, sleekly iced white cake needs only a few tiny, colorful flowers to make an impact.

THE RIGHT BAKER

or out, accompanied by a photo), time, number of guests, and style of reception (tea, luncheon, sit-down dinner, buffet, formal, informal). Your budget is essential.

For the more creative element of the conversation, most bakers want to get a sense of a bridal couple's personality, which makes it very important that all meet in person before any decisions are made. In addition to the basic information detailed above, be prepared to offer descriptions of the type of decorations (flowers, fabrics, colors, favors) planned for the reception, details and style of the bridal and bridal-party dresses, headpieces and any other flourish that is part of the bridal ensemble (including shoes!), if and what family wedding traditions will be part of the celebration, and whether there is anything about your relationship that may possibly be used in the design of the cake. Some couples prefer to reference the place where the proposal was made, while others are eager to display their profession (usually if it's shared) or a passion for a specific animal, sport, or hobby in the design of the cake. The possibilities are limitless.

Tiered, Layered, or Sheet—Which Style Suits Yours?

A wedding cake can be anything you want it to be—contemporary, dramatic, ornate, regal, simple, or homespun. Perhaps you've long dreamed of an all-white wedding, from your dress and flowers to the traditional, dreamy, three-tiered wedding cake, filled with buttercream and covered in white icing. Now that the day is almost here, the traditional tiered cake seems a bit too ordinary, or perhaps it doesn't fit with the casual mood you want to create.

The style of your wedding will also influence the shape and, more importantly, the structure of your cake. For an at-home luncheon for forty, an elaborate tiered cake is hardly necessary or appropriate, whereas an extravagant ballroom wedding lends itself beautifully to a towering cake. A round, tiered cake is tradition bound while a square stacked cake reflects a more contemporary style. A heart shape—

Opposite: Be sure to discuss the cake stand with your cake designer. This silver stand fits seamlessly under a classic white cake, enhancing its simple elegance.

though a cliché—is perhaps the perfect expression of your wedded bliss.

While some couples choose cake shapes that reflect an event or cherished memento—a famous monument where they were engaged, a beloved pet, an icon of their profession—the more conventional shapes and structures include: heart, rectangular, petal, hexagonal, round, square, sheet, separated tiers, stacked tiers, and satellite cakes. Discuss the style and setting of your wedding with your cake designer and ask him or her which shape will best convey the mood you're trying to achieve. Then ask to see photographs of the cakes he or she thinks would fit well in your setting.

How Much Cake Do I Need?

Every baker has a different idea of how many servings they can cut from a cake. The numbers vary slightly from baker to baker, due to each one's flavor options, so it's important to ask how many guests each tier will serve. For example, a dense, dark chocolate, nut, or fruitcake would generally be cut into smaller slices than a light, airy yellow sponge cake filled with buttercream or fresh fruit. Generally speaking, wedding cake slices, for a 3- to 4-inch-high cake tier, are approximately ¾ inches wide by 2 to 2½ inches deep. Also, square tiers provide more servings than round/petal/hexagonal tiers. Three tiers will serve 50 to 100 guests; you'll likely need five layers for 200 guests or more.

Some cake designers will suggest a cake size that will serve all of your guests in addition to a small tier that is traditionally saved for your first anniversary (see page 103). Don't be tempted to underestimate the number of slices of cake you will need. Internationally renowned cake designer Ron Ben-Israel warns, "I once had a client tell me that there were 100 fewer people on her guest list than she had invited. Someone had suggested to her that trimming the size of the cake was a good way to save money. As a result, the servings of cake were very small, embarrassing the caterer and more importantly, the bridal couple."

Opposite: *A square cake is modern and fun; especially when several tiers are stacked like presents one upon the other. The sea-inspired decorations here, especially the kissing sea horses, echo the lighthearted mood of this cake, and couple.*

Cakes and Weather

In general, warm weather presents the most risks for wedding cakes. Whether iced with fondant, buttercream or meringue, a wedding cake should never be placed in direct sunlight. Fresh flowers will wilt, decorations may slide, and worse, buttercream cakes and chocolate decorations are at great risk of melting. Some decorations, such as pulled/blown sugar, crystallized flowers, and some gum-pasted decorations, can start to melt or look "tired" on very humid days. What's more, they are at risk of melting if they are stored in a refrigerator, as that too is a humid environment. A seasoned baker can tell you what ingredients, materials, and decorations are weather resistant in the venue you've chosen and how to keep the cake safe until you're ready to cut it.

Don't be tempted to underestimate the number of slices of cake you will need.

Once you have decided on the baker who's right for you, it's time to ask some essential questions.

How much do you charge per serving for the basic cake offered?

Do you deliver and set up the cake?

Is there a cost for this?

How will the cake be delivered?

Who will cut the cake?

Who is responsible for returning the cake stands and any other related items owned by the baker?

Do you have other cakes to deliver on the same day of my wedding?

Can you give me two or three references?

Then call every reference on the list before you make your commitment.

Opposite: Serving each wedding guest a single petit four is a charming alternative to a slice of cake. For a small, supremely elegant gathering, place each one under glass and garnish with fresh flowers.

CAKE TALK—A GLOSSARY OF TERMS

You don't need to have a professional's knowledge of baking in order to envision your dream wedding cake, but it may give you confidence to know some of the basic terms associated with cakes and, more specifically, wedding cakes, when you meet your baker.

Basket weave—A piping technique that echoes the interwoven reeds of a wicker basket, best achieved using buttercream and royal icing.

Buttercream—A light, creamy frosting made with butter, confectioners' sugar, egg yolks, and milk or light cream that stays smooth and soft and can be colored and flavored easily. It is used to render lifelike flowers, swags, and any decoration that can be piped. Buttercream can also be spread spotlessly smooth to create a perfectly flat surface on which to arrange decorations.

Cake tower—A multilevel, multiarmed cake stand used to display individual cake layers that surround the main cake.

Columns—Also known as pillars, columns are de rigueur in most traditional tiered wedding cakes. Tubes are placed between each tier to achieve open air between each of them. Unlike separators, columns are clearly visible and are part of the overall design of the decorated cake.

Cornelli—An intricate piping technique that yields a lovely lacelike design.

Dacquoise—A circular dessert consisting of layers of meringue mixed with ground toasted nuts and layers of whipped cream mixed with soft fruits.

Dotted Swiss—A piping technique in which tiny raised dots are arranged in patterns on the cake to resemble dotted-Swiss fabric.

Piping

Basket weave

Dragées—Sugar-coated almonds that come in a variety of sizes and colors, including silver and gold. They are used primarily for decorative purposes.

Filling—A fruit- or cream-based "paste" spread between layers within tiers of a wedding cake.

Fondant—A sweet, elastic confection used for both candy and icing, it is made of sugar-water and cream of tartar cooked to the soft-ball stage. It is extremely pliable and is literally rolled out with a rolling pin and draped over a cake. Fondant is excellent for achieving precise, architectural designs and decorative details.

Ganache—A classic chocolate and cream mixture that bakers use for many chocolate applications, from fillings and glazes to truffles. It has a very shiny, smooth finish.

Genoise—A classic European sponge cake. It is a tender but dry cake that is usually moistened with a flavored sugar syrup.

Groom's Cake—An old custom that is still observed at some weddings, a groom's cake is a separate cake, traditionally fruitcake but more increasingly chocolate cake. It is usually served along with the wedding cake and cut into slices and packaged for guests to take upon leaving the reception.

Gum paste—This mixture of sugar, cornstarch, and gelatin can be molded like clay and turns hard and brittle as it dries. It is used to mold realistic-looking fruits and flowers to decorate a cake. While not as flavorful as marzipan, gum-paste decorations are edible and can be stored for years as keepsakes.

Latticework—A piping detail that consists of crossed strips arranged in a diagonal pattern of open spaces.

Columns

Groom's Cake

Marzipan—A sweet, pliable paste made of ground almonds, sugar, and sometimes, unbeaten egg whites that is used to mold edible flowers or fruit to decorate the cake. It can be tinted and molded into almost any shape and can also be rolled in sheets, like fondant, and used as icing.

Meringue—A mixture of egg whites, sugar, and air that is whisked and dried in a slow oven. Meringue can be shaped before drying.

Piping—Decorative details, such as borders, basket-weave patterns, and flowers, created by forcing frosting through a pastry bag equipped with various metal design tips.

Pulled sugar—A technique in which boiled sugar is manipulated and pulled to produce flowers and bows.

Royal icing—Made of egg whites and confectioners' sugar, this icing starts life as a soft paste piped from a pastry bag to create latticework, beading, bows, and flowers. When dry, its texture is hard and brittle. Do not refrigerate.

Sugar dough—A mixture of confectioners' sugar, water, cream of tartar, and tragacanth gum that can be molded like clay and turns hard and brittle as it dries. Often used for cake decorations. It is also known as *candy dough* or *gum paste*.

Torte—A dense cake that does not use leavening agents like baking powder or baking soda.

Whipped cream—Heavy cream beaten until soft and foamy. It is unstable and not recommended for outdoor weddings.

Cake tower

Marzipan

Royal icing

CHAPTER 4

Flavors and Frills

Remember how many wedding-dress styles you looked at before you chose the one that seemed like it was made just for you? When you first put it on, it made you glow on the inside and the outside? Your wedding cake should have the same impact; it should be as deliciously memorable on the inside as it is stunningly beautiful on the outside. The only rules that should influence your decision are that your cake must taste delicious and that it be big enough for everyone to enjoy a piece.

Flavor is as important as all the visual elements of your wedding; it makes an indelible imprint on memory. However, it needn't be overwhelming. A plain cake that tastes wonderful will be as well remembered as a visual stunner elaborately embroidered with pulled-sugar flowers. Flavors have personalities, too, so try to use the ones that reflect the mood of your wedding: Chocolate is decadent; vanilla, luscious and pure; spices, autumnal; lemon, sprightly and tart.

What's inappropriate? A wedding cake can be any flavor you want it to be, as long as the cake itself, the filling, and the icing are harmonious. "The ultimate test is if the cake simply doesn't taste good," says baker Wendy Kromer. "That, and if it doesn't stand up to being stacked or decorated as you'd like." She suggests that white or yellow cake can be combined with just about any filling and icing, while chocolate cake is best with chocolate, praline, mocha, or vanilla buttercreams; chocolate ganache; and raspberry, strawberry, or orange fillings.

Nut-based cakes are well suited to fruity fillings and creamy icings. Christine Deonis, a New England cake baker, says chocolate cake with mocha filling and mocha buttercream icing is very delicious, while lemon pound cake with any kind of berry filling is equally successful. She advises against ice cream cakes and combining chocolate cake and lemon filling.

Page 60: Flowers made from piped frosting can be as beautiful as the real thing. Roses in various stages of glorious unfolding add an exquisite flourish to this tiered white cake.

Above and opposite: If the fresh version of your favorite flower is out of season or isn't safe to place on the cake, you can still have it made out of buttercream, a very versatile medium for rendering almost any decoration imaginable, in any color. Here purple and white frosting lilacs are piped onto a charming chocolate layer cake.

Special Touches

Cakes can also be decorated to provide a clue as to the flavor on the inside. For example, gum-paste orange blossoms can adorn a cake of orange chiffon layers spread with citrus curd. If you've decided on a cake covered with white chocolate ganache with fresh strawberry puree between the layers, you can provide a clue as to the flavors on the inside by artfully arranging marzipan wild strawberries round the tiers. If apricot jam separates the layers of your cake, why not surround your cake with the delicately colored fresh fruit.

SENSATIONAL FLAVOR COMBINATIONS

lemon pound cake with lemon mousse filling and vanilla buttercream

chocolate layer cake with chocolate filling and white chocolate fondant icing

applesauce or spice cake with cream cheese filling, dusted with confectioners' sugar

almond genoise and dacquoise layer cake filled with buttercream and iced with Swiss meringue buttercream

maple layer cake with maple buttercream filling and icing

carrot cake with buttercream filling and icing

coconut cake with lemon curd or strawberry puree filling and seven-minute frosting

lemon poppy seed cake with fresh lemon curd and lemon mousse topping

red velvet cake with white-chocolate cream cheese filling and frosting

croquembouche: cream puffs filled with pastry cream, stacked into a triangular tower, and bound in a web of whisper-thin strands of lightly caramelized sugar

cheesecake covered in fondant, buttercream, or marzipan

The trick to choosing just the right additional decorations is to express the style you've envisioned for this sweet celebration. Among the most popular flourishes are gum-paste or marzipan fruit and flowers. Piped buttercream decorations are also frequently chosen by bridal couples, either for making handsome or playful borders around the tiers, for creating an overall pattern on all of the tiers, or for rendering their favorite flowers, birds, pets, or china patterns on their wedding cake.

Sugared fruits such as kumquats, crab apples, seckel pears, champagne grapes, and strawberries; leaves, herbs, and edible flowers glisten when gently arranged on a wedding cake. Dragées and gold leaf, too, can add the sparkle of silver and gold for a dramatic effect. Royal icing is an excellent medium for making delicate, long-lasting decorations; it can be used both to make fanciful patterns and to attach them to the cake, as it dries very hard. Of course, seasonal fresh fruit, flowers, and nuts will never go out of style, especially if they are artfully set atop the cake.

Opposite: Wild strawberries, fashioned from tinted marzipan, sprout from the tiers of a fondant-covered cake— an elegant contrast to stark white. The tiny berries also offer a visual hint that the filling is strawberry flavored.

Page 66: Sugared seckel pears and plums are arranged as if in a still life painting. On a smooth canvas of fondant they exude a simple elegance.

Topping It Off

The top of the cake is usually reserved for the pièce de résistance: a traditional ceramic bride and groom figurine, fresh or faux flowers or fruit, an elaborately tied marzipan bow, or grandmother's vintage cake topper. The options for cake toppers are unlimited, but the reigning favorite is fresh flowers. Some bridal couples prefer a bare cake top, especially if their cakes are minimalist and sleek. If you are set on a bride-and-groom figurine but can't find just the right one, your cake designer may offer to render one out of marzipan or may be able to lead you to someone who can.

"My favorite cake topper is 'something borrowed'," says cake designer Ron Ben-Israel, "like an antique bride-and-groom figurine that has been passed down through the family." Ben-Israel also suggests opting for something made out of sugar—swans, a castle, a keepsake ornament, and even a tiara. A rather handsome—and poignant—way to crown a wedding cake is with the initial of your new last name, made from fresh herbs wrapped along a wire letter or piped in royal icing. Some of the most poignant cake toppers are not brand new but old. Scour your mother's and grandmother's attic or china cabinet for a charming and suitable family heirloom. "Something old" is never inappropriate on your wedding day.

Page 67: *Some brides think baroque is best and can have it tastefully translated onto their wedding cakes. Buttercream flourishes and a looping crown look smart set atop this slick white cake. Sugared grapes with their leaves intact provide a lush base and topper.*

Opposite: *A frisky bouquet of tiny white blooms makes a lovely finishing touch to a square cake. The openwork basket-weave frosting recalls a garden trellis.*

Left: *Cake toppers can be almost anything, but the classic porcelain bride and groom will never go out of style.*

Page 70: *An heirloom bride and groom stand tall beneath a trellis of stephanotis on a towering four-tiered confection.*

Page 71: *Buttercream vines grow up from the base of a tiered cake, leading the eye to a porcelain bride gracefully dressed with a veil of real lace.*

Above: *A wedding in the woods inspired this multitiered basket-weave cake. The unusual—and humorous—brown bear topper is perfectly suited to the setting.*

What It Will Cost

The most successfully planned weddings begin with a well-laid-out budget with the cost of the cake claiming from 3 to 5 percent of the total amount you plan to spend on your celebration. This is the average amount, though some couples choose to trim costs in other areas in order to boost their cake budget. In most cases, the cost can be determined as soon as you decide how many guests will be attending and what kind of cake you want; cake designers price their cakes by the slice, and the costs range widely depending on where you live and what kind of cake you desire. In urban areas such as Atlanta, New York, and San Francisco, the base price may begin at $3 per slice or even more if you use a highly sought-after cake designer. The rates can range from $1.50/slice for a basic white or yellow cake with buttercream frosting to $15.00/slice for a dense chocolate and nut cake covered in fondant with marzipan decorations.

Keep in mind that your choice of cake and frosting flavors will have comparatively less impact on price, as baking ingredients are relatively inexpensive. What really drives up costs are any handmade decorations, intricately molded shapes, and precise decorative details that require long hours to create. When you discuss prices with the cake designer, inquire about delivery and accessory rentals and whether you will be charged extra for the top tier—the one traditionally saved for the first anniversary (see page 103). Be aware that many cake designers require a 25 to 50 percent deposit.

FLAVORS AND FRILLS

While your budget may dictate a simple cake, unceremoniously iced, there are many clever ways to trim the cost of your fantasy confection. With a little ingenuity and knowledge gained before visiting your cake baker, chances are good you can keep expenses down and still have the perfect cake on your wedding day. Consider using the staff pastry chef of the hotel, country club or catering service you have chosen rather than hiring a cake designer; you'll avoid cake-cutting fees, additional tips, and delivery costs.

Choosing fresh flowers for decorations and selecting buttercream for your icing are among the most frequently recommended cost-cutting tips. Forget about feeling that you're compromising: buttercream is delicious and nothing brings a cake to life more than fresh blooms. If you can't imagine forgoing your fantasy cake but can't possibly afford the high per-slice cost, ask your cake designer to make a small version for display and the ceremonial cake cutting then have him or her make backup sheet cakes for serving guests. If the reception space requires a towering cake in order to stand out, discuss having a cake arranged satellite style with your baker. A satellite cake gives the illusion of height and breadth with a top layer of separate cakes tiered on top of a lower layer of separate cakes. Square tiers generally provide more servings than round tiers, though they can be more time consuming to construct and frost.

If money is no object and you've allotted a larger-than-average portion of your budget to the cake, then let your imagination run wild. Molded flowers and fondant icings are among the most expensive choices, with the lifelike flowers driving the

CAKE WISE
"I urge people to be very direct. If there is a budget issue, be up-front about it. You can't stretch something that isn't there. Let's say you can't afford a cake designer. Bringing a picture from a magazine to your local bakery and asking them to re-create it from the photo is not very realistic. Look at the cakes they've done successfully. Simplify. Keep it elegant and fun rather than creating a disaster."
—Ron Ben-Israel, cake designer, New York City

price per slice as high as $5 to $10. Royal-icing flowers fall somewhere between fresh and molded, resulting in a $3 to $4.25 slice of cake. Depending on the flavors you choose, requesting a variety of cake flavors—a different one for each tier, for example—will increase the cost of your cake. If a multitiered square cake is your idea of the perfect wedding confection, expect to pay more for the labor involved in getting those tiers to line up perfectly and the icing to turn the corners without flaw.

Before you depart from your meeting with your cake designer, review each point in the contract. Don't be afraid to ask for specifics, including details as to which display items or cake accessories must be returned and what the charges are for failure to do so. Together you should create a precise description of the cake you've agreed upon and include that description in the contract. For example, clarify what "a three-tiered, fondant-covered cake decorated with gum-paste flowers" really means. Gum-paste flowers covering every tier? Cascading in a spiral from top to bottom? Or just ten scattered about? Ask your cake baker to discuss the ingredients he or she uses; whipped cream and Cool Whip are toppings with very different tastes. Don't hesitate to get the specifics; your baker will appreciate the clarity and so will you.

Choosing fresh flowers for decorations and selecting buttercream for your icing are among the most frequently recommended cost-cutting tips.

THE BAKER'S CONTRACT
As with all of the vendors who will supply professional services for your wedding, your baker should provide you with a contract for services you have both agreed upon. The contract should contain the following points:

Date of contract

Name and contact information, including cell phone numbers for the vendor and you

Wedding date, time, and location (be specific)

Detailed description of the cake (design, flavor, fillings, icing type, decorations, number of tiers, shape, topper, number of slices)

A list of items you're renting (plastic tiers, cake stand, columns) and how they should be handled after the wedding

If anything inedible (fresh flowers or greenery, gum-paste flowers that may have wires in them, plastic hardware) is used on the cake, it should be VERY CLEARLY stated in the contract and provisions made for what should be done with those items before serving the cake.

Delivery and setup fees

If the baker is responsible for decorating the cake table, a description of the decorations and the additional fees charged.

Total price

Deposit amount

Balance and due date

Cancellation and refund policy

Cake designer's signature

Your signature

Opposite: Eye-popping displays of five "satellite" cakes surround a slender cake tower. Dowels divide the cake tiers, making room for luxurious bunches of roses and stephanotis. The monochromatic scheme is interrupted by only one color: the green leaves, which "loosen" the look just perfectly.

CHAPTER 5

Cake Presentation

From Fun to Fabulous

At the ceremony, it is the bride who is the focal point, her beaming face and graceful stance accentuated by her dress, veil, flowers, shoes, and jewelry. At the reception, the main object of the guests' visual attention is the cake, and its structure and decorations should be enhanced by a distinctive presentation. Once you've determined what your cake will look and taste like, it is equally important to discuss with your baker how it will be presented. The possibilities range from the traditional—an elaborately decorated round cake table—or the unconventional—a stone birdbath for a garden wedding.

One couple who was married in an art gallery set their square, three-tiered cake on a pedestal, as if it was a sculpture on exhibit. Another couple celebrated their union in a big barn in Connecticut in which the cake was set upon towering bales of hay! The wedding cake can also be the centerpiece of a dessert buffet, stylishly arranged in the center of the table, surrounded by bowls and platters of varying heights (none ever higher than the cake) filled with candies and confections. If your style is playful yet elegant, you might set multiple cakes atop the arms of an appropriately sized plant stand.

Not all cakes need elaborate presentations or luxuriously dressed tables. A multi-tiered chocolate cake—a version of the layer cake your grandmother used to make frosted with broad strokes of buttercream—calls for nothing more than an equally charming painted bistro table with a "distressed" finish. One of the simplest ways to dress a cake table is to casually scatter the same kind of flowers that appear on the cake around its base. This is most successful if the flowers are long lasting. Alternatively, arrange tiny vases filled with flowers around the base of the cake for a simple decorative touch.

Take your presentation cues from the cake shape, color, and decorations. It should complement the design, stature, and style of the cake. For example, if a favorite childhood quilt inspired the piped decorations on your cake, clothe the table with fabric—similar in design and texture— or in the very quilt itself. If you are serving a traditional white cake, you can't go wrong with a pristine white tablecloth. Another option is to incorporate the colors of the bridal flowers or bridal-party dresses into the table decoration.

For some couples, the cake is as important as every other element of the wedding. If it is to you, as it was to one Connecticut couple, then by all means draw extra attention to it. One half of this bridal couple was an architect who designed and built a separate tent for the cake. He wanted to be sure

Page 76: *A beribboned cake stars at a reception in the living room. Dessert dishes, teacups, champagne glasses and petit fours seem casually strewn on the round table, but they are in fact artfully arranged to frame the stunning cake.*

Opposite: *Cake and champagne follow a casual evening ceremony at home. A playful polka-dot cake, rimmed in bright green buttercream leaves and set on a milk-glass cake stand, is long on charm and informality.*

Page 80: *Perhaps the simplest way to decorate the table on which the cake is presented is with heaps of fresh blossoms. Just be sure they don't touch the cake if they're not edible.*

CAKE WISE

Ron Ben-Israel is not a fan of elaborately decorated cake tables. He believes the cake should really be the focus. If the cake is grand in and of itself, then there's no need for embellishment. When he is considering how to present the cake, Ben-Israel follows the example of great couturiers. "When clothes are made from the best fabrics and are cut to perfection, there is almost no need for accessories," he says. "If a cake is made from the best ingredients, has structural integrity and wonderful decoration, then that's enough."

all of the guests saw the cake and so designed the tent in such a way that the guests had to walk around the cake in order to enter the reception.

Beware the precarious presentation of the cake, however. Ron Ben-Israel recalls the wedding reception that took place in a large home with a sprawling staircase. The bridal couple asked that the cake be set on a table on the landing so that guests could see it as they walked in. The bride's young nephew was so taken with the sight of the cake on entering the party that he ran up to it and hugged it, leaving his face imprinted on the tiers. The good-natured bride was charmed, and the cake was served with laughter all around.

Below: *A snowy coconut cake is perfectly suited to a wedding celebration at home; it needs nothing more than a white linen tablecloth to make an impact.*

Cutting the Cake

Centuries before there were elaborately decorated, tiered cakes and ribbon-wrapped silver cake knives for slicing, the wedding "cake" was represented by barley bread, a symbol of the bride's fertility. The groom would eat a piece of the bread and break the remainder of the loaf over the bride's head, symbolizing the taking of her virginity and his dominance over her. Today, the tradition of "breaking bread" together has evolved as much as the original wedding "cakes" have. While today's cakes are still made of flour, a form of wheat, wedding cakes

can still be considered a symbol of the bride's fertility—or of a new life. But participating together in the ritual of cutting the cake represents a couple's commitment to share life's tasks and whatever paths their life takes.

Depending on the style of your wedding, cutting the cake can be reserved for the end of the reception or just before dessert is served. At a sit-down dinner or luncheon wedding, the cake is usually served immediately after dinner. At a buffet dinner, it is traditionally cut and served just before the reception ends. For a traditional cake-cutting ceremony, the groom puts his right hand over the bride's right hand and together they cut the first slice from the bottom tier of the cake. Sometimes they cut two slices, in order to feed each other a small bite. The cake is typically removed to the kitchen, where it is sliced and served to guests.

As wildly varied as wedding cakes can be, the ritual of cutting them has remained as tradition bound as the exchange of wedding bands. While some bridal couples today choose not to participate in the cake-cutting ceremony, the majority of brides and grooms find it as poignant as the exchange of vows. In this, your first shared task as a married couple, make a few special arrangements in advance to ensure that the ceremony is as joyous as possible. Designate a family member, or rely on your wedding planner if you are using one, to ask the bandleader or emcee to make a gentle announcement at an agreed upon time for the cake cutting ritual. If you have arranged for the cake cutting to take place with dancing and socializing time to spare after-ward, remind that same family member to tell the band to begin playing right after you feed each other a bite of cake.

According to tradition the cake should be cut just before dessert at a lunch or dinner reception and shortly after guests arrive for a tea or cocktail reception. A ribbon-tied silver knife is the traditional utensil to use. (This is never used to cut slices for guests: it's too thick to make precise cuts.) If you registered for a silver cake knife and have already received it, by all means use it. You may even want to have your

Opposite: A veritable rose garden surrounds a wedding cake displayed at an outdoor reception. The cake table should always be set out of the way of heavily trafficked areas—and safe from curious pets and little ones.

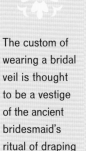

The custom of wearing a bridal veil is thought to be a vestige of the ancient bridesmaid's ritual of draping a cloth on the bride's head before the bread was broken over it.

initials engraved on it before your wedding day. An heirloom, such as the knife your parents used on their wedding day, is also a lovely choice.

Once the announcement has been made the bride and groom should stand just to the side of the cake. The groom should place his right hand over the bride's, and together they should cut into the bottom layer. Traditionally, the bride and groom feed each other a taste of the first slice as a symbol of their willingness to share a household. Some couples today have dispensed with this part of the ritual, while others find it poignant and symbolic. However you decide to share your cake with each other, it is never appropriate to stuff each other's mouths with cake. Once the cake is cut and shared between the bridal couple, it is removed to the kitchen where it is cut and served to guests.

Songs for Cutting the Cake

There isn't a bride and groom in the world who wouldn't love the chance to have two, three, or even four first dances as a married couple. Perhaps it is the very public performance of a very personal sentiment that makes it so exhilarating. A music-filled wedding can have a powerful impact on you and your guests, providing memories that will be remembered long after the last bit of cake is eaten. Why not choose a favorite song for the band or disc jockey to play when you cut the cake?

This ritual, too, is a public affirmation of your commitment to each other, and a favorite song can only add to the poignancy of the moment. Unlike the song you chose for the first dance, this song needn't be one you can comfortably dance to! Review the list of songs you considered for your first dance and reconsider those you thought inappropriate for the waltz or boogie. Chances are, there is a perfect accompaniment to the cake-cutting ceremony. Dinner music is also appropriate when cutting the cake.

Opposite: Cutting the cake is as much a part of the wedding ritual as the cake itself. The bride and groom hold the handle of the knife together, symbolizing their first shared sustenance of married life.

How to Cut a Tiered Cake

Most caterers have cut dozens of wedding cakes of all shapes and styles. Chances are they will not need any instruction on cake cutting. On the other hand, if friends or family are throwing your party, a bit of guidance may be needed in order to get the right number of slices from the cake. Be sure to have an apron, a thin, long knife, a spatula or cake server, and, if the icing is Crisco based, a warm wet towel to clean the knife between cuts. A stack of plates and enough forks and napkins for every guest should be close by.

The first step in serving the cake is to remove the top tier and the armature used to hold it up. This tier is traditionally saved for the couple's first anniversary (see page 103). If there is no anniversary tier, remove the top tier and set it aside, followed by each remaining tier. If your cake topper is an heirloom or has sentimental value and can be preserved, be sure to instruct your caterer to give the topper to one of your attendants for safekeeping. Begin cutting slices from the bottom tier. For a 16-inch round tier, make an impression of a circle about 4 inches from the rim of the tier using the sharp knife. Cut through the impression. Beginning with the outer circle, cut ¾-inch-thick wedges from the outer rim; you should have about twenty-four slices of cake. As you cut, hold the knife in one hand and a cake server in the other. Allow the slice to fall onto the cake server, then slide the slice onto the cake plate. Cut the remaining ring of the tier into twelve slices, each about ¾ inch wide. Continue cutting the smaller tiers in this manner, until you reach the smallest tiers, which can be cut like a regular layer cake. If the bottom tier is larger than 16 inches, make a second circle within the first and proceed as described above.

How to Serve the Cake

Custom dictates that it is bad luck for a guest to leave the reception without tasting the wedding cake. To preserve all of the good fortune that a wedding day promises

Opposite: A long thin knife is best for cutting the cake. You will also need a cake server to catch the slices and slide them onto plates.

(and to guarantee that nobody misses out on every element of your delicious cake), follow a few simple guidelines for serving the cake. For a sit-down luncheon or dinner, the bride and the groom and the bridal party are served first. The guests seated at tables closest to the bridal party table are then served, followed by the remaining tables, with the servers working their way out to the tables on the edge of the room.

If your cake is covered in edible molded decorations, is served with a sauce, or is accompanied by ice cream, be sure to review this with the caterer or family. Are there enough marzipan flowers to place two on each slice of cake? How big should the scoops of ice cream be? A dry run is a good idea: You can use a stand-in cake and decorations to determine these details in advance.

For a buffet-style reception, there are several ways to serve the cake. Often the slices are set out on a large buffet table, and guests are invited to help themselves to cake once the bride, groom, and bridal party have sat down to eat theirs. Another option is to serve the slices as you would for a sit-down luncheon or dinner, progressing from the bridal table on to the guests' tables. This works especially well for an informal wedding, in which guests are encouraged to circulate freely from table to table and dance as they wish after dinner.

Above: Wedding cakes are generally sliced in wedges, with care taken to include part of the decoration on every plate.

Emergency Fixes

Professional cake designers never have emergencies; it is their business to ensure that no matter the circumstances, your cake is perfectly presented at your wedding reception. They do take preventive measures, however, and always have an emergency repair kit on hand. Wendy Kromer feels the best way to ensure that her cakes arrive perfectly is to deliver them herself. She carries extra decorations, icing, a pastry bag and whatever piping tips have been used, a spatula, Swiss army knife, dowel cutter, towels, and aprons. She uses these tools to put the final touches on the cake, once it has been placed on the cake table. In addition to spatulas, cardboard, dowels, and extra decorations and icing, Christine Deonis brings a small knife with a pointed tip to remove any stray matter that may float onto the cake during delivery.

CAKE WISE

"My most spectacular emergency occurred in the early days of my career. I offered to make the cake for my friends' wedding in New Hampshire," recalls Wendy Kromer. "My plan was to make the cake in New York City, then drive it all the way to New Hampshire. I designed a tiered cake, each one separated by one inch of space. The cake was completely finished and well refrigerated, and quite pretty, I might add, when I put it in my rented car, a hatchback. I arrived four hours later at the B&B where I was staying with the bride, opened the hatchback to find the cake had warmed up and the dowels inside had loosened. The car had shifted slightly, of course, during the drive, causing the cake to collapse on itself! I cancelled my invitation to the rehearsal dinner that night "due to my desire to put the finishing touches on the cake." I was up until 4:30 A.M., salvaging what tiers/flowers I could and baking a few new tiers. I only brought one tip with me, as that was the only tip I used on the original cake. Thank goodness the couple running the B&B were sympathetic souls and gave me full run of their kitchen. The saving grace of the whole fiasco? When I saw my friend walk down the aisle in her reworked vintage wedding gown, I couldn't help but notice that the design I created on her cake with that one tip, matched the design of the lace in her gown perfectly."

If the homemade cake lovingly made by your aunt did not survive the trip from her house to the reception intact, consider setting up the cake table in such a way (a corner, alcove, or up against a wall) as to help camouflage the damage. Position the cake with the perfect side facing the guests and the damaged side toward the wall. If a cake becomes runny from sitting out too long before the cutting ceremony, remove

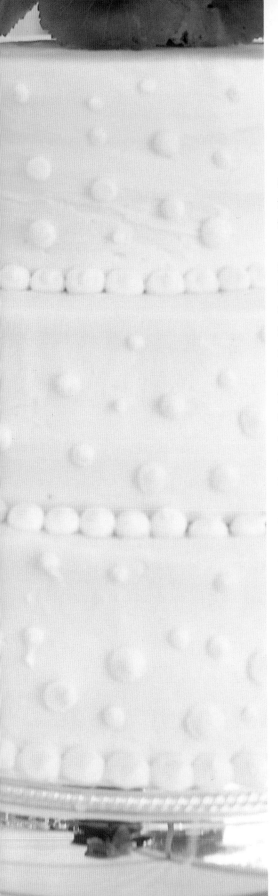

It is said that
unmarried guests
who place a piece
of wedding cake
under their pillow
before sleeping
will increase their
prospects of
finding a partner
and bridesmaids
who do likewise
will dream of their
future husbands.

any perishable decorations and place only the runny tiers in the freezer for up to twenty minutes.

Preventing emergency fixes is far easier than patching up a cake that has slid off its base, or redecorating an entire cake that has melted before the reception. In general, the wedding cake should be delivered to the reception space just as it has come out of the refrigerator. An air-conditioned car will preserve the chill on the ride to the reception space. If the cake baker is traveling a great distance, it is wise to ice, decorate, and arrange the tiers at or in a space close to the reception (see Cake Wise, on page 89).

Common sense dictates that the cake table be placed out of reach of wandering dogs and curious children, away from hot lights or large windows that throw direct sunlight. Appoint a friend or member of the bridal party to check on the cake periodically. Give him or her the authority to decide what actions should be taken if, in fact, the cake has sustained serious damage during the reception. If it begins to slide, fall, or seems to be in a precarious position, ask the caterer to remove it from the reception floor.

Left: *The wedding cake is always a great source of curiosity, and it is always charming to see a wide-eyed child stand before the cake. But a stray finger is less so. Put one of the bridesmaids in charge of checking on the cake while it is displayed at the reception.*

Photographing the Cake

Most wedding photographers will ask you for a
list of pictures that you want them to take on
your wedding day. From the scurrying of the
bride and her attendants getting dressed for the
ceremony to the fanfare surrounding the bridal
couple as they leave the reception, there are
iconic images of every wedding day that should
always be captured on film. Your wedding cake
is one of them.

CAKE WISE
Christine Deonis recalls
the one big scare she had
while delivering a cake.
"A car ran a stop sign and I
had to slam on my brakes.
The tiers shifted, but the cake
did not fall over, thank God.
Thanks to my emergency kit,
I was able to repair it to its
original beauty."

Laura Moss, a wedding photographer based
in New York City, says that she photographs the cake whenever she can. She arrives
at the reception space well before the ceremony begins, if the cake is scheduled to be
there. Moss suggests coordinating the timing of the cake photograph with the cake
designer or caterer. Much of the decision as to when she photographs the cake
depends on where the cake is placed. Sometimes it is set in a separate room, the easiest instance in which to get a great photograph.

She generally shoots many versions: the whole cake including the table, tight
shots of the whole cake and decorative details, as well as shots of the couple cutting
the cake. If the cake is beautiful when sliced, she will take a picture of a plated piece.
"If the cake is in a setting that isn't particularly beautiful, I go in tight and try to cap-
ture just the cake itself in the photograph," says Moss. Natural light results in the
most beautiful images of wedding cakes; she suggests making considerations for the
photograph of the cake when determining where it will be presented. If the cake is
placed in a very dark space, she finds that candlelight placed around the cake results
in very beautiful pictures. "I never like to set up lights at a reception; they're unat-
tractive and are easily knocked over."

Opposite: *When photo-graphing the cake, take a
variety of angles, including
distance shots as well as
close-ups. You don't want
to miss a setting as
beautiful as this one.*

CHAPTER 6

Grace Notes

At the reception, as in married life itself, it is the small, sweet gestures that make a difference. Among the easiest—and most charming—ways to create a unique and memorable wedding day is to present your guests with a tiny memento to take away. The custom of delighting guests with wedding favors, as they have come to be called, has its roots in Southern tradition, when the groom's cake, once exclusively a fruitcake, was sliced and placed in monogrammed boxes for each guest to take home.

It used to be that only unmarried girls received a piece, in order to place it under their pillows in hopes that the man they dreamed of would become their future husband. The groom's cake disappeared for several decades but is now making a strong comeback in flavors and styles as varied as the wedding cake itself. It is always smaller than the wedding cake—one or two tiers at most—but no less fanciful in its appearance. Chocolate cakes are very popular today, as are cakes rendered in the shapes of the groom's favorite hobbies or pastimes. The groom's cake is generally ordered from the wedding cake designer. They do not, however, provide the tiny boxes for transporting each slice. Be sure that you have provided these for the caterer to box the tiny slices.

Edible favors are always well received, and are not limited to tiny slices of the groom's cake. Anything sweet—candy-coated almonds, iced cookies, tiny chocolates, petit fours—is appropriate. Packaged and presented in your own style, these traditional favors become unique to your wedding. Favors don't have to be limited to food; the only rules to remember are that they must be small enough to carry in your hand and be available in multiples.

As you've done for your flowers and food, take cues from the season for your favors. A small tree ornament is a sweet keepsake from a Christmas wedding, tiny gourds filled with flowers are lovely at an autumn wedding, and foil-covered chocolate turkeys are charming for a Thanksgiving wedding. A garden wedding might inspire tiny bouquets of just-picked flowers whereas a spring-

Page 94: Love is everywhere at a wedding—even in the confections. These heart-shaped cookies are whimsically decorated with royal icing and set in a dish, one for each table.

Right: *For the groom who is a star grill master, why not a cake to call his own? A groom's cake can be as whimsical as the wedding cake; it is usually chocolate and somewhat smaller in scale.*

Opposite: *Modern grooms' cakes often reflect the passions of the husband-to-be. This playful rendering of jumping trout would make any avid fly fisherman's heart beat faster.*

Page 98: When selecting the table sweets to enhance your cake, think about what to serve them in. This beautiful glass dish shows off the tiny frosted cookies to perfection.

time celebration is the perfect time to give your guests seedlings to plant in their own gardens and remember your special day. Perhaps the area in which you are being married lends itself to great favor ideas. A wedding in rural Vermont begs to showcase pretty bottles of maple syrup, whereas a ranch wedding in Texas brings red bandannas to mind.

The presentation of favors is another chance for you to put your personal stamp on your wedding day. Arrange them in a place that guests will be sure to pass by on their way out the door, or ask the caterer to set one on each place setting before guests arrive at the reception. Favors can also be passed. Give the job to the small flower girls and any young boys participating in the wedding. This bit of theater will charm guests, and the children will be happily occupied.

A word of advice on choosing your favors: The cost of a tiny memento may seem inconsequential to your wedding budget, but when you multiply it by 200 people, you can burst your budget fast. The costs include the favor itself, its

Page 99: A romantic– and edible–lovebird rendered in meringue makes a wonderful dessert to serve at a small celebration. Meringues should always precede the serving of the cake.

Right: *Cookie plates are often set on each table as the cake is being served. Ask your caterer to box those that have not been eaten to give to guests as they leave.*

Opposite: *For true lovers of sweets, a candy table is as important as a fabulous cake. Dragées, the symbol of fertility and the bittersweet nature of love and marriage, are set on a table alongside tea and champagne.*

packaging, and presentation. Many bridal couples make their own favors or gather their friends in the months before the wedding to help them assemble their tiny gifts. If you are having difficulty finding a special item in bulk, look on the Internet; there are plenty of wedding websites with excellent sources for all manner of favors.

Cookies and Candy for the Table

A wedding cake is always awe-inspiring enough to stand on its own, but surround it with glistening dishes, bowls, and compotes full of variously shaped candies and confections, and its presence is majestic. Cookies and candy are never expected at a wedding reception, making them a cause for pure delight for guests young and old. No matter the sweets you choose, the key to presenting them beautifully without stealing the spotlight from the wedding cake itself is to place them in vessels of varying heights, none higher than the wedding cake. The cake should be placed in the center of the table, with the footed bowls, plates, and compotes surrounding it. The taller vessels in the back and on the ends; and middle-height and low dishes in front.

While there are no rules as to what confections to choose, following some general guidelines will guarantee a beautiful table. Choose sweets that are no bigger than one or two bites. Ideally, they will not clash, colorwise, with the wedding cake. For example, a traditional white wedding cake can be flanked by all-white sweets served in white dishes for stunning impact. Tiny white chocolates, dragées, white gumdrops, divinity fudge, coconut macaroons are all delicious white confections to consider.

GRACE NOTES

On the other hand, pastel-colored candies set in silver dishes would beautifully complement a formal white cake. Many bridal couples want to have their favorite sweets at their wedding. The groom's favorite cookies, made in miniature, and the bride's favorite penny candy, can be cleverly presented in pretty stacks and in elegant footed bowls to give them wedding cake table cachet.

Savoring a Sweet Memory

Today, tiered cakes are sized to feed all of the guests at the wedding reception. But in the days when three tiers covered in white frosting was the only appropriate style, each tier assumed a specific role. The bottom tier was served to guests at the reception, the middle tier was sliced and packaged for guests to take home, and the top tier was reserved for celebrating the christening of the first child. While the reason for saving the top tier has changed, the practice has not. Today, it is often shared on the couple's first anniversary to celebrate the happy memories of the wedding day.

Many cake designers will include the top tier of the cake in the price of the cake; the remaining tiers are large enough to feed all of your guests so that you can save the top tier for your first anniversary. Ron Ben-Israel suggests the best way to preserve your cake is to refrigerate it until it hardens. Ask your baker which decorations can be saved. Sugar decorations can last for months and months, while marzipan, which contains almond oil, can be refrigerated up to three weeks. Wrap the tier in several layers of plastic wrap—do not skimp on the plastic—and freeze. The cake can be frozen up to a year and still taste good, says Ben-Israel, as long as it is made from pure butter. Any other fat used will break

> While there are no general **rules** as to what **confections** to choose, following some **general guidelines** will guarantee a beautiful table.

Opposite: Instead of giving a slice of cake to departing guests, consider petit fours made in the same flavor and frosting. The tiny jewel-like cakes will keep better than a slice because they haven't been cut.

down slowly over the course of the year, imparting an "old" flavor to the cake.

The night before your anniversary, bring the cake gradually to room temperature by placing it in the refrigerator. Remove it from the refrigerator the next day, unwrap and bring to room temperature. Whether you've saved the tier of your actual wedding cake or re-created a tiny version on your anniversary, what better way to celebrate the sweet taste of love and marriage than with a symbolic slice of wedding cake.

Opposite: *A small sweet makes a wonderful parting gift for guests, especially when inscribed with a personal message.*

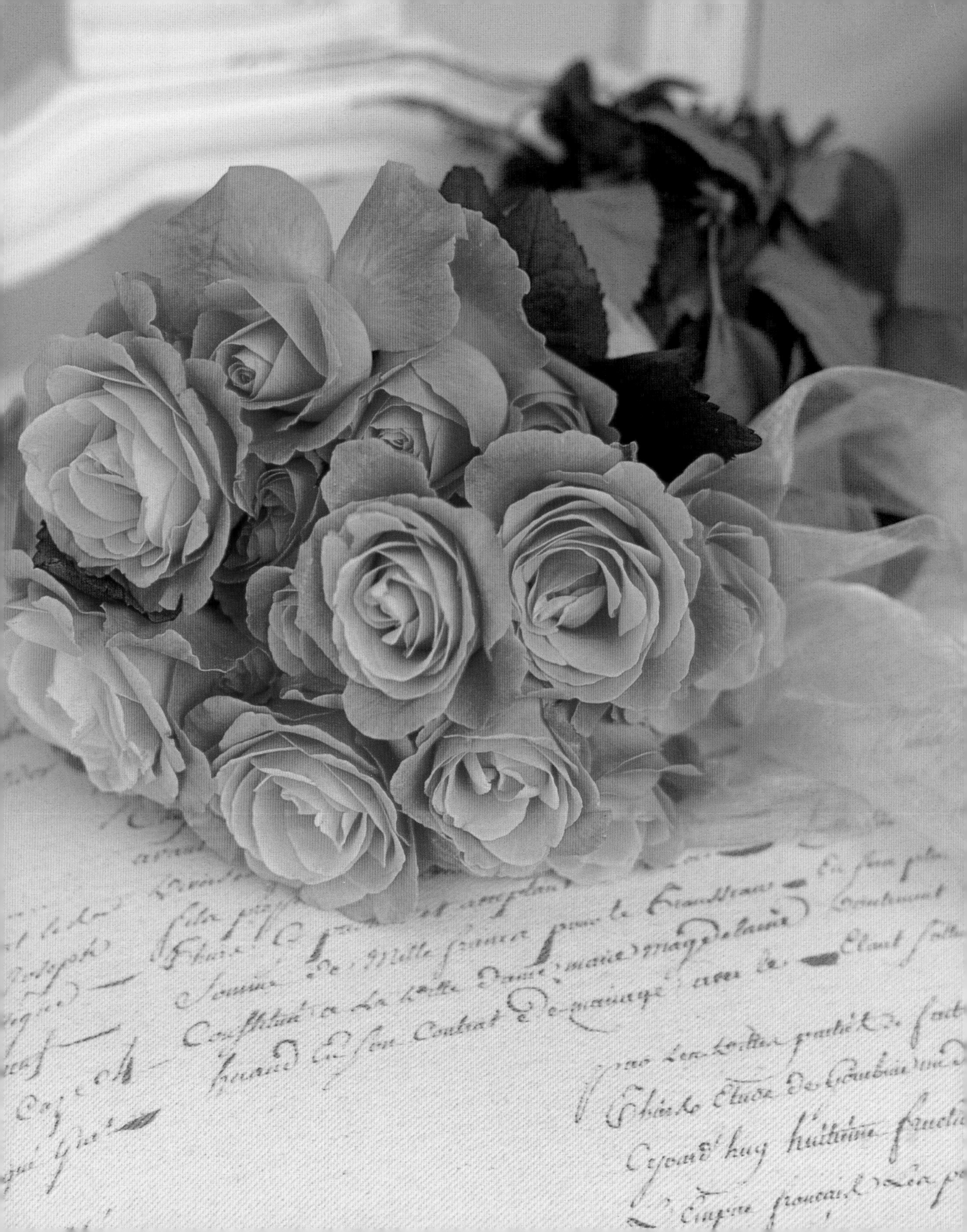

Part II
Wedding Flowers

Flowers are Love's truest language.

—Park Benjamin, *Sonnet*

Introduction

"The wedding day. . . should stand out in the calendar, bright with all the brightness of love and gratitude." Well over one hundred years after these words first appeared in a popular nineteenth-century women's magazine, your wedding day still represents one of the most important milestones of your life, one you'll look back on with fondness for years to come. Even today, it represents the ultimate fantasy—sparkling rings, long white dresses, fresh flowers perfuming the air, your first dance together as husband and wife—all while being surrounded by family and friends, beaming with joy.

The **first thing** any bride should know about wedding flowers is that they may very well be *the* key consideration in determining the "look" of your wedding.

Like every bride, you naturally want everything about the day to be personal and unforgettable. And whether you're planning an intimate wedding breakfast, a simple buffet, or a formal reception, much of the special charm and romantic atmosphere of your wedding will come from your choice of flowers.

As you go through these pages, you'll find that wedding flowers are much more than mere decorative accessories. Indeed, it's their freshness and vitality that will help you create an event that everyone will remember with pleasure forever. From your own precious bridal bouquet and the flowers for your wedding party to the floral adornments at your ceremony and the centerpieces at your reception, their colors, fragrance, and beauty can help transform your wedding day into a magical and momentous occasion.

Opposite: *A bouquet of dahlias in brilliant scarlet tones accented with a few pink blooms is a richly romantic and dramatic choice.*

Armfuls of wildflowers and rustic baskets filled with yellow tulips and daisies, for example, immediately call to mind a country wedding. If you've always dreamt of a wedding with a romantic medieval or Victorian theme, you'll likely choose fragrant wreaths of herbs (so suggestive of those days of chivalry) or roses and lacy ferns densely clustered in a nineteenth-century-style bouquet. Specific styles will help give your wedding the period flavor you're looking for. For one celebrity wedding, a renowned floral designer was inspired to re-create the fairy-tale ambience of a glittering turn-of-the-century Russian winter, with a stunning cathedral aisle canopied by twenty-foot snowy white birch trees. Glittering blue lights amidst a "snowfall" of thousands of white flowers pinned to the branches cast an enchanting glow over the ceremony.

In some cases, an affinity for a certain type of flower becomes the theme for the entire wedding. Case in point: the bride-to-be who woke in the middle of the night when a vision of lush, old-fashioned pink roses suddenly appeared in her mind. Absolutely everything, she decided—except for her dress of pure white—would feature those marvelous pink roses, from her bouquet, wedding stationery, and rose-patterned bridesmaids' dresses to minute details like a bit of delicate rose-ribbon trim on her junior bridesmaid's ballet-slipper-style shoes!

On the big day, her dream was realized. Pink roses lavishly embellishing pew ends and doorways greeted guests as they entered the church. At the reception, bowls of pink roses surrounded by twinkling votive candles, long-stemmed roses tucked into folded napkins, and velvety pink petals scattered on tables created an ultraromantic effect. As a crowning touch, even the canapés were flower shaped!

If you're like most brides, though, the prospect of choosing your wedding flowers can be daunting. Unless you routinely order bouquets by the dozen and floral centerpieces for dinners of two hundred, you're soon going to be buying more flowers for one single day than you probably have bought in your entire life! On the other hand, of the myriad decisions you'll face as you progress with your wedding plans, few will be more delightful and fulfilling than deciding on the flowers that best express your love. The very act of planning your wedding flowers tends to give you the opportunity to think about all the tender "little things" that can make a wedding truly unique, from learning what different flowers mean and selecting delicate floral favors for your dearest girlfriends to choosing just the right boutonnieres for the lapels of your husband-to-be and his groomsmen.

So, on the following pages, we're going to demystify the wedding flower process for you. You'll find information on gathering ideas, working with a florist, photographs of traditional (and nontraditional) bouquet styles, a gallery of popular wedding flowers, and much, much more. Plus, we'll take a look at all the many special floral extras that can make your wedding day personal and turn your fantasy into a beautiful reality.

Opposite: Charmingly old-fashioned, this posy is composed of lilies of the valley and grape hyacinth.

CHAPTER 7

Flowers, Flowers Everywhere

Flowers are an integral part of your wedding. Chances are you've heard this before, but what does it really mean? To determine that, before you even think about sitting down to talk with a florist, let's consider all the ways, large and small, that flowers enhance—and sometimes actually create—the style and atmosphere of your wedding day.

When people think of wedding flowers, three things generally come to mind: a bridal bouquet, flowers for the wedding party, and the centerpieces. What could be so complex about that? In fact, there are far more opportunities for floral decorations and accessories than you may realize. Most brides today, for example, top their wedding cakes with fresh flowers instead of the conventional plastic bride and groom figures. Cakes themselves are often nestled in a bed of delicate greenery; perhaps a few rosebuds are twisted around the handle of the cake knife that the couple will use to cut the first slice. The bride may want a circlet of traditional orange blossoms to attach to her veil. Or a floral tiara. Or even elegant garland-style headpieces made up of white roses and deep purple anemones for her bridesmaids. Your florist will supply all of these things.

Perhaps you'll need artful greenery and fresh blossoms to transform your reception hall, church, temple, or party tent into a French country garden or Elizabethan fantasy. Or a bower of flowers to decorate a Victorian gazebo. The possibilities are endless. One bride revived a charming old custom she read about in a nineteenth-century etiquette book: A bridesmaid, holding a straw basket filled with long-stemmed flowers, stood at the door of the church handing out flowers to guests as they arrived for the ceremony. Another designed a striking *huppah*—the wedding canopy used in traditional Jewish ceremonies—created entirely from flowers. Perhaps your old college roommate, favorite cousin, or fiancé's parents are coming in from out of town and staying at a local hotel. Many florists will deliver flower baskets coordinated with your wedding theme to their hotel rooms—an especially warm, welcoming touch to greet them when they arrive.

Finally, don't forget about all the surrounding celebrations and events that may call for flowers: bridal showers and engagement parties, wedding breakfasts and rehearsal dinners, your bridesmaid's luncheon, and more.

That's not to say you *must* do all or any of these things. Remember, it's your wedding and your own personal choice. But knowing what the different options are will help you determine how and where you want to feature flowers on your wedding day.

Page 112: *There are more than three thousand varieties of roses. A traditional and romantic choice, roses work well with any style of wedding.*

Wedding Flowers Checklist

Use this checklist as an organizer to help you keep track of the flowers
you'll need to order and to help you remain within your budget.

PERSONAL FLOWERS	Quantity	Flower Varieties or Arrangement Style
Bouquets		
Bride	_____	_____
Bride's Tossing Bouquet	_____	_____
Maid/Matron of Honor	_____	_____
Bridesmaid(s)	_____	_____
Junior Bridesmaid(s)	_____	_____
Flower Girl(s)	_____	_____
Boutonnieres		
Groom	_____	_____
Best Man	_____	_____
Groomsmen	_____	_____
Ushers	_____	_____
Father(s)	_____	_____
Ring Bearer(s)	_____	_____
Stepfather(s)	_____	_____
Grandfather(s)	_____	_____
Special Guests	_____	_____

PERSONAL FLOWERS	Quantity	Flower Varieties or Arrangement Style
Corsages		
Mother(s)	_____	_____
Stepmother(s)	_____	_____
Grandmother(s)	_____	_____
Special Guests	_____	_____
Hair Ornaments		
Bride	_____	_____
Maid/Matron of Honor	_____	_____
Bridesmaid(s)	_____	_____
Junior Bridesmaid(s)	_____	_____
Flower Girl(s)	_____	_____
Ceremony		
Entrance	_____	_____
Railing Garlands	_____	_____
Pew/Chair Decorations	_____	_____
Altar Arrangements	_____	_____
Huppah	_____	_____
Petals for Flower Girl	_____	_____
Tossing Petals	_____	_____
(for bride and groom's departure)		

PERSONAL FLOWERS	Quantity	Flower Varieties or Arrangement Style
Reception		
Entryway Arrangements	_____	_____
Place-Card Table Arrangements	_____	_____
Head Table Arrangements	_____	_____
Centerpiece Arrangements	_____	_____
Buffet Table Arrangements	_____	_____
Bar Decorations	_____	_____
Restroom Arrangements	_____	_____
Cake Table Decorations	_____	_____
Wedding Cake Decorations	_____	_____
At-Home Weddings		
Entryway	_____	_____
Mantel Decorations	_____	_____
Window Treatments	_____	_____
Staircase	_____	_____
Home Altar	_____	_____
Chairs	_____	_____

Special Touches

Flowers for Hotel Rooms for Wedding Party and Other Guests

Flowers for the Rehearsal Dinner

Flowers for Decorating the Grill of the Bridal Car

Thank-you Bouquet for the Bride's Parents

Thank-you Bouquet for the Groom's Parents

CHAPTER 8

Getting Started

Traditional or contemporary? White roses or yellow tulips? Gardenias, pansies, freesia, or lilacs? Unless you're a horticultural pro or gardening expert, how do you go about selecting the flowers that best express your personal style?

The first thing to realize is that your choice of flowers *is* personal—there is no right or wrong when it comes to wedding flowers, nor are there any rules you *must* follow. If there is a flower that has a special meaning to you and your groom—perhaps he brought you yellow daisies on your first date—then by all means incorporate it into your wedding theme. Are you worried that using flowers other than traditional pastel-colored blooms will look odd and inappropriate? Perish the thought! Yes, soft yellow, creamy white, and delicate blush-pink blossoms are traditional because they *do* look beautiful at weddings (next to white, even today, pink is still the most popular color for wedding flowers). But so do less conventional, more dramatic shades of scarlet, blazing orange and apricot, cobalt blue, deep wine-red, and other vibrant colors that have become fashionable in recent years. So express yourself. The point is, on this day, your flowers are an expression of who you are and how you see yourselves as a couple. Be as romantic, playful, imaginative, or offbeat as you wish.

Of course, that's not to say there aren't some guidelines to help make your choices easier. While the *style* of your wedding flowers is strictly personal, the month in which you're planning to be married, where you live, your budget, and other factors play a significant part in your final choices.

Arrangements that reflect a contemporary point of view usually use fewer types of flowers and feature a single type in each bouquet.

Expressing Your Personal Style

Think about the weddings you've attended, and chances are your favorites, the ones that stand out in your mind as memorable or moving, are not the biggest, most fashionable, or most extravagant, but rather those that have a certain, elusive "something extra." They don't simply mimic the latest trends or reproduce some designer-of-the-moment's style, but somehow manage to express something personal about the wedding couple's taste and style.

So when it comes to flowers, how do you select those that reflect your personality, your style, and your view of life? That's where your florist comes in. On meeting a new bride-to-be, he or she may make note of certain visual clues to get a sense of your personal style (how you dress, for example, or wear your hair or makeup). He or she may ask you questions about the type of décor you favor, and your reactions to different fragrances (more brides are taking fragrance into account when choosing flowers). But, often, color is the most important element: Your florist will ask you what color flowers you envision (all-white, shades of pink, red, yellow, and orange, etc.) and then tell you what flowers are available in that particular color.

What your wedding gown looks like will also help the floral designer zero in on the

Page 118: Tulips are available in a wide range of colors, including white, pink, yellow, red, magenta, and purple. They work well for both formal and casual weddings.

Opposite: This bride is carrying a whimsical parasol composed of yellow oncidium orchids. Floral touches in imaginative and unusual forms such as this parasol can make your special day even more memorable.

GETTING STARTED

right flowers for you. If you've always dreamed of floating down the aisle in yards of satin or filmy tulle, with the requisite "something old, something new, something borrowed, and something blue," accordingly, your florist may suggest formal, elegant arrangements of lilies, roses, orange blossoms, and starry bunches of stephanotis. Are you getting married in a slim gown with sleek, modern lines and favor a "less is more" style of décor? So it should be with your flowers—perhaps orchids and arum lilies in cool, spare, Asian-influenced arrangements.

Of course, no one is suggesting you confine yourself to such neat, cookie-cutter categories of "romanticist," "traditionalist," and so on. Most personalities are too complex and eclectic for that. That's why, as you work with your florist, you'll find it is not so much the actual flowers that are important, but how they look together that counts.

The following tips will help you visualize your style in terms of flowers.

The same flowers can express different moods, depending on variety, color, and form. Pink-, peach-, or champagne-colored roses and looser blooms say romantic while Black Magic roses (a velvety, mysterious dark red), vibrant hues, and tighter blooms may feel contemporary or sophisticated, depending on what they are paired with.

Arrangements that reflect a contemporary point of view usually use fewer types of flowers and feature a single type in each bouquet.

Traditional arrangements have a greater variety of different types of flowers per bouquet and often are placed in antique-style or silver containers. A typical combo: all-white or pastel-colored flowers—peonies, calla lilies, sweet peas, and ranunculus.

Loose, unstructured arrangements of flowers with long stems and stalks (such as delphiniums) and old-fashioned, unpretentious flowers like daisies, tulips, cornflowers,

Opposite: Even the family pet can get in on the action. Here, a loyal Labrador stands ready to lead the bridal party to the altar at this home wedding. The color of the dog's collar has been color-coordinated with the hue of the roses.

BIRTH MONTH FLOWERS

January: Carnation
February: Violet
March: Daffodil
April: Sweet Pea
May: Lily of the Valley
June: Rose
July: Larkspur
August: Gladiolus
September: Aster
October: Calendula
November: Chrysanthemum
December: Narcissus

lavender, and Queen Anne's lace suggest a country or garden mood. For bouquets, consider a sheaf style, brimming with berries and herbs. **For an ultraromantic feeling**, go for lush profusions of varied blooms in velvety textures and brilliant colors or monochromatic arrangements. **Choosing flowers by fragrance** can be a lovely idea; that way, whenever you smell lilacs or lavender or gardenias, for example, you'll be reminded of your wedding day. Freesia, roses, gardenias, lilacs, lilies, tuberoses, hyacinths, violets, lavender, and sweet peas are among the most fragrant flowers. If scent is important to you, be aware that while many new hybrid flowers are beautiful, they often have very little or no scent at all.

Practical Considerations

Once you've considered your personal style, you'll have to think about practicalities. Various factors, especially seasonal and budget considerations, may play a role in your choice of flowers, affecting the varieties you choose, the colors, and the quantities.

Seasonal Availability

In the past, brides were restricted to choosing flowers that were in bloom only in their particular area at that particular moment. In fact, many florists still urge you to consider seasonal availability when it comes to wedding flowers. It's not a bad idea, either. There's still something to be said for the freshness and suitability of flowers

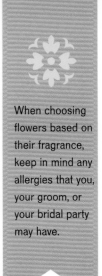

When choosing flowers based on their fragrance, keep in mind any allergies that you, your groom, or your bridal party may have.

that are evocative of the season at hand. Not convinced? Imagine attending a wedding in steamy August where pots of brilliant red poinsettias and boughs of holly line the bridal aisle. Or delicate daffodils and daisies at a wedding on a chilly November eve. Even to a floral novice, these combinations seem unnatural and incongruous, don't they? That's why taking into account some degree of seasonal availability simply makes good sense.

Seasonal availability means more than knowing that tulips bloom in the spring, peonies blossom in May or June, and sunflowers are easier to come by in late July than in deep December. It also depends on local climate. Frosty white roses, mistletoe, and evergreens might sound perfect for a December bride—but only if she lives in New England, not Hawaii. If your wedding is in the summer (or you live in a hot, humid climate all year round), you'll be better off forgoing fragile flowers like gardenias, lilies of the valley, tulips, and wildflowers, for hardier blooms that won't wilt, like sunflowers, zinnias, hydrangeas, and dahlias.

If you have an unlimited budget and can fly in, from anywhere in the world, any out-of-season flower or exotic bloom that strikes your fancy, then by all means,

Left: *In this classic round bouquet, pale pink parrot tulips add a whisper of color to the creamy white French tulips.*

indulge! But if budget is a consideration, you'll quickly realize that locally grown, seasonal flowers will be a lot kinder to your pocketbook. Out-of-season flowers such as imported orchids or white peonies in February will need to be specially ordered and can cost up to three or four times as much as flowers that are locally grown, and some florists insist they find locally grown blossoms fresher than ones that need to be specially ordered. One florist who emphatically prefers local seasonal blooms to forced, hothouse flowers put it this way: Nature produces its best naturally.

But what if there is one exotic or out-of-season flower that you simply have your heart set on for your wedding. If so, go for it—you can cut floral corners elsewhere by going with seasonal greenery and local flowers for everything else. And remember, some flowers—ivy, roses, and evergreens, to name just a few—are year-round favorites and are always stylish, beautiful, and appropriate for weddings.

Although your local florist is your best guide to what flowers are obtainable where you live, this list will give you some general guidelines as to seasonal availability.

Spring: tulips, amaryllis, bluebells, mimosa, lily of the valley, calla lilies, daffodils, forget-me-nots, anemones

Summer: sunflowers, baby's breath, lavender, larkspur, carnations, Queen Anne's lace

Spring to Summer: iris, orchids, clematis, freesia (to late summer), foxglove, gardenias

Summer to Fall: hydrangea, snapdragons, heather, dahlias, delphinium

Spring to Early Fall: stephanotis

Fall: hydrangea, calla lilies in fall colors, fall roses, pansies

Late Spring to Early Summer: peonies, ranunculus, rosemary, lilacs, magnolias (spring to midsummer)

Winter to Spring: camellias, hyacinth, paperwhites, narcissus, daffodils, sweet pea

Opposite: *Tulips, pansies, and a large calla lily anchor this loosely arranged sheaf-shaped bouquet of white flowers. While a sheaf shape can be very formal, the mix of flower varieties here gives the bouquet a freshly picked feel.*

Calculating Costs

Next to the cost of your reception, your flowers are probably the most expensive item in your wedding budget. As a general rule, whether your wedding costs $5,000 or $50,000, experts advise setting aside about ten to fifteen percent of your overall wedding budget for flowers.

Of course that's just an average, which means that as many people spend more as spend less. If flowers are especially important to you and you've always envisioned yourself surrounded by masses of fresh blooms on your wedding day, you'll want to apportion more money to flowers and less to other areas.

But what do they cost? Before you sit down with your florist, do a little homework on how specific items are priced. Depending on the style, size, and types of flowers you want (and where you live), bridal bouquets can be priced anywhere from $75 to several hundred dollars each. Large or dense arrangements with more flowers or with exotic or out-of-season blooms will obviously cost more.

The list below will help you estimate some typical costs for flowers for your ceremony and reception. Prices will vary from region to region and depend on your choice of flowers, their arrangement, and seasonal availability.

Bridal bouquet: $75 and up
Bridesmaid bouquet: $40 and up
Floral hair wreath: $35 to $100
Corsage: $5 to $25 and up
Boutonniere: $5 to $10
Flowers for your ceremony: $100 to $500 per arrangement
Reception centerpieces: $80 to $250 and up
Floral huppah: $250 to $3,000

Opposite: *A single strong color—romantic yellow in this case— makes a lush bouquet and a big impact.*

Blooms on a Budget

Following are some strategies to help you keep costs down:

Smart scheduling: When you're choosing a wedding date, remember that flowers (especially roses) are pricier around Valentine's Day, Mother's Day, and other holidays when flowers are more in demand in general. On the other hand, if you are getting married over a holiday, your church already may be decorated with Christmas holly and poinsettias, or Easter lilies, which can cut down or even eliminate the cost of ceremony flowers. You may need only to adorn the pew ends (or the last chair in each row) with ribbon and tulle. The same thing holds true if your ceremony is outdoors, in a park, garden, or on the beach; extra flowers may not be needed at all.

The time/labor factor: Often, it's not the flowers themselves but the florist's labor and time that increase the cost. So think twice about small but potentially expensive details (floral napkin rings that need to be individually wrapped around each napkin, for instance).

Keep it simple: Instead of formally arranged bouquets made with different types of flowers, consider having your bridesmaids carry a simple nosegay or a single flower or two (one perfect calla lily, a sunflower or orchid, a few tulips, or a large-headed rose). At the reception, loose flowers in vases will cost less than elaborately arranged centerpieces.

FLOWERS: WHO PAYS FOR WHAT?

The rule is . . . there are no rules. But if you're following tradition, the bride's family pays for ceremony and reception flowers, and flowers for the bridesmaids and flower girl. The groom pays for the bride's bouquet, although the flowers are chosen by the bride. The groom also pays for boutonnieres for himself, his father, best man, and ushers, and for corsages for his mother and the bride's mother. Corsages and boutonnieres for grandparents on either side are a nice gesture, though not strictly traditional. They, too, are paid for by the groom. The bride's father's boutonniere is traditionally ordered by and paid for by the mother of the bride.

Fool the eye: Use inexpensive flowers and greenery like baby's breath and ivy to add fullness to skimpy bouquets and arrangements. Herbs also will add fullness, texture, and fragrance. A bouquet of fresh mint, rosemary, and marjoram will not only look wonderful, but will also smell wonderful.

Double up: Let bridesmaids' bouquets do double duty. Glass vases placed on the cake table or guest-book table can hold bridesmaids' bouquets at the reception and save you the expense of additional centerpieces.

Far left and near left: Some brides opt to include beaded flowers in their bouquets. This exuberant bouquet includes roses in the palest shade of pink, white peonies, and a few delicate beaded flowers.

Recycle: After the ceremony, have the altar flowers and decorations moved to your reception (pew decorations can be draped on doors or buffet tables; altar arrangements on the dais or cake table). Similarly, if you're having a wedding brunch the next morning, consider reusing the reception centerpieces. Otherwise, have them delivered to the hotel rooms of out-of-town guests so they can continue to be enjoyed, or donate them to a hospital, community shelter, retirement home, or charity event.

Use interesting containers: Choose containers and vases that look pretty with just a few select flowers, rather than elaborate, costly arrangements. Consider rustic wooden boxes or terra-cotta pots instead of cut-glass vases, or scour flea markets, thrift stores, and tag sales for interesting unmatched vintage vases at minimal cost. Be creative: For a country wedding, for example, try a cluster of glass tumblers, old-time preserving jars, or glass milk bottles filled with flowers on your tables. Discount shops can also offer up attractive surprises—and bargains—such as milk glass vases, small pitchers, and the like.

Add accessories: Let accessories add ambience to your reception tables without upping costs. Supplement small or simple flower arrangements with votive candles, candlesticks in varying heights, baskets of moss, and bowls of fruit and nuts.

Break 'em away: Arrange small pots of flowering plants together to form what are known as "breakaway" centerpieces. Afterward, guests take them home as wedding favors.

Watch the whites: White flowers may be traditional, but they cost more than colored flowers. Because white flowers bruise easily, your florist will need to buy more than are called for to replace any that may be damaged from handling.

Your Ceremony and Reception Sites

Spend some time at the sites you've chosen for the ceremony and the reception. Do you want to highlight their special features (especially if the architecture of the

Opposite: Utilitarian objects can be used in witty new ways. Simple or quirky containers, for example, from nurseries, tag sales, or even hardware stores make attractive, original, and affordable centerpieces for the bride on a budget. This small galvanized-steel tub brimming with flowers makes an ideal centerpiece for a casual summer wedding.

Right: *For an old-
fashioned touch, why
not have two flower girls
walk down the aisle
carrying a garland?
The garland hangs
gracefully between each
flower girl and is held
at the ends by handles.*

venue is designed in a particular architectural style, such as Arts and Crafts or English Tudor), or transform them completely? A reception at your local country club may require a lot of flowers to enliven a humdrum room, whereas a grand hotel ballroom may call for just a few elegant arrangements. If your wedding will be held outdoors, the beauty of the site may be enough to set a romantic mood; in that case, you might just need a few floral decorations at the outdoor "altar."

Gathering Ideas

After you've locked in your wedding date, it's a good idea to start a wedding notebook. Most brides choose a scrapbook-style journal in which to paste or tape pictures or an oversized loose-leaf binder set up with dividers and zippered inserts to hold fabric swatches and sundries. Unless you're highly knowledgeable about flowers, you may not be able to describe the type of arrangements you envision, or even identify the specific flowers in a bouquet you've fallen in love with. But having photographs of flowers or arrangements you like is a great way to help your wedding planner or florist effectively hone in on the mood and look you want.

In your notebook, then, set aside a section designated "Flowers" and start collecting ideas. Tear out pictures that appeal to you from magazines; include photographs of place settings, centerpieces, and bouquets that you like (or ones you don't). Collect suggestions for floral favors that seem unique, ideas from other weddings you've attended, and more. Talk to your friends (especially those who are recent brides) about weddings they've attended where the flowers were especially notable.

Over the next few weeks, assembling these examples will give you some familiarity with the subject. At some point, you may notice a common thread in the type of flowers you're drawn to, be it color, texture, or overall style. Perhaps your pages are filled with simple, loosely arranged flowers with a "just-picked-from-the-garden" look, as opposed to formal, elaborately wired arrangements. Try to keep a small camera in your purse when you're going out shopping or attending another event (it doesn't have to be a wedding); you never know when you'll pass a store window or attend a party that has a centerpiece or flower arrangement you want to remember.

ANEMONE
Season: November–May
Colors: white, pink, purple, magenta, burgundy
Cost: moderate to expensive
Scent: none

ASTER
Season: November–May
Colors: white, yellow, pink, purple
Cost: moderate
Scent: none

AMARYILLIS
Season: November–April
Colors: white, green, yellow, pink, red, burgundy
Cost: moderate to expensive
Scent: none
(the belladonna variety, shown here, has a mild fragrance)

Popular Wedding Flowers

To help you familiarize yourself with the countless varieties flowers come in, following is a visual guide organized in alphabetical order. This is not a complete list; rather, it highlights flowers that are popular for weddings. Each flower has its own special qualities, whether it's color, shape, or fragrance. As you browse through these pages, you'll see old favorites and discover new ones, and you'll gain a better sense of which blooms appeal to you.

CALLA LILY
Season: year-round; peak is winter to late spring
Colors: ivory, yellow, orange, pale pink, dark pink, red, burgundy
Cost: expensive
Scent: none

CANTERBURY BELLS

Season: June–October

Colors: white, blue, purple, pink

Cost: expensive

Scent: none

CHRYSANTHEMUM

Season: year-round; peak in late summer and fall

Colors: white, yellow, green, orange, russet, red, burgundy

Cost: inexpensive

Scent: musky

CAMELLIA

Season: late winter to early spring; fall

Colors: white, cream, pink, red

Cost: inexpensive to moderate

Scent: sweet

CORNFLOWER

Season: summer to early fall

Colors: white, pink, blue

Cost: inexpensive to moderate

Scent: none

COSMOS

Season: midsummer to fall

Colors: white, pale pink, dark pink

Cost: inexpensive to moderate

Scent: none

DAFFODIL

Season: spring or fall

Colors: yellow, white, apricot, orange

Cost: inexpensive to moderate

Scent: sweet or none

DAHLIA

Season: summer to early fall

Colors: white, yellow, orange, pink, red, purple

Cost: inexpensive

Scent: strong and spicy

DAISY

Season: summer to early fall

Colors: white

Cost: inexpensive

Scent: none to faint

DELPHINIUM

Season: year-round; peak is June–October

Colors: white, lavender, pink, blue, purple

Cost: moderate to expensive

Scent: none

DUTCH TULIP

Season: November–May

Colors: white, yellow, orange, pink, red, purple

Cost: inexpensive to moderate

Scent: none

FORGET-ME-NOT

Season: May–September

Colors: white, blue, pink

Cost: moderate to expensive

Scent: none

FREESIA

Season: year-round

Colors: all colors except blue

Cost: moderate

Scent: sweet

FRENCH TULIP

Season: November–May

Colors: ivory, pale yellow, pink

Cost: expensive

Scent: none

GARDENIA

Season: year-round

Color: ivory

Cost: expensive

Scent: fragrant

GERBERA DAISY

Season: year-round

Colors: white, pink, yellow, orange, red

Cost: moderate

Scent: none

GLADIOLUS

Season: year-round; peaks during the summer

Colors: white, yellow, green, apricot, orange, pink, red, lavender, purple

Cost: inexpensive

Scent: none

GRAPE HYACINTH

Season: November–May

Colors: white-green, blue-purple

Cost: moderate to expensive

Scent: sweet

HYACINTH

Season: November–May

Colors: white, yellow, pale pink, peach, fuchsia, lavender, purple, blue

Cost: moderate

Scent: very sweet

HYDRANGEA

Season: July–November

Colors: white, green, pink, burgundy, purple, blue

Cost: moderate to expensive

Scent: none

IRIS

Season: year-round; peaks in spring to early summer

Colors: white, yellow, purple

Cost: inexpensive to moderate

Scent: none to sweet

LILAC

Season: spring

Colors: white, pale pink, dark pink, lavender, purple

Cost: moderate to expensive

Scent: strong and sweet

LILY

Season: year-round; peaks in spring and summer

Colors: white, yellow, apricot, orange, dark pink, red, purple

Cost: moderate to expensive

Scent: none to strong; depends on variety

LILY OF THE VALLEY

Season: year-round; peaks in spring

Colors: white

Cost: expensive

Scent: fragrant

PEONY

Season: spring

Colors: white, cream, peach, pink, burgundy

Cost: moderate to expensive

Scent: sweet to aromatic

PHLOX

Season: June–November

Colors: white, pink, red, purple, orange

Cost: moderate

Scent: sweet and mild

ORCHID

Season: year-round

Colors: white, yellow, apricot, orange, green, pale pink, dark pink, red, burgundy

Cost: moderate to expensive

Scent: none to fragrant; depends on variety

RANUNCULUS

Season: November–April

Colors: white, yellow, apricot, orange, pink

Cost: moderate to expensive

Scent: mild

ROSE

Season: year-round

Colors: white, cream, yellow, apricot, orange, pale pink, dark pink, red, russet, burgundy, lavender

Cost: moderate to expensive

Scent: none to very fragrant

STEPHANOTIS

Season: year-round

Colors: white

Cost: expensive

Scent: slight

SUNFLOWER

Season: May–November

Colors: deep gold, orange, russet, brown, pale lemon

Cost: moderate

Scent: none

SWEET PEA

Season: November–June

Colors: pink, lavender, white, cream, apricot, red, purple

Cost: moderate to expensive

Scent: very sweet

VERONICA

Season: year-round

Colors: white, pink, purple

Cost: inexpensive to moderate

Scent: none

ZINNIA

Season: June–September

Colors: yellow, green, orange, pink, red

Cost: inexpensive

Scent: none

CHAPTER 9

Finding a Florist

When you've reached the point where you have some ideas about the types of flowers you want, the next step is to find a floral designer who can help you achieve your vision. This is the person who will provide all the personal flowers for your wedding as well as create the floral decorations for your ceremony, reception, and any other parties too. Top floral designers and wedding planners are often booked months in advance—sometimes more than a year. (Remember: There are only fifty-two weekends a year and even the most accomplished can only handle so many parties on each weekend.) Be sure to give yourself plenty of time—at least six months to a year before your wedding date—to find a person with whom you're comfortable, who is both creative and able to work within your budget.

If you're not working with a wedding coordinator, the best way to find a talented floral designer is by word-of-mouth. Talk to recently married friends and ask relatives or coworkers for their recommendations as well. If you're at a wedding or other

Page 144: A bouquet of roses is a classic choice for a bride. This loosely composed arrangement has a fresh, "just picked" look.

event and think the flowers are fabulous, don't be shy: get the florist's name from your host. Your caterer or reception site manager will have worked with many different florists and often can provide recommendations (anyone they know is likely to be familiar with the wedding site too).

Once you have a few names, ask for Web sites where you can view samples of their work. Many florists will post photographs of different bouquets, centerpieces, and other treatments they have done, so you can immediately get a sense of their style and learn something about their business too. One thing you'll want to learn is how much of their business involves weddings; that way, you know they'll be familiar with any situations that may occur and be able to handle the unexpected. But don't just rely on pictures. Be sure to get references from the florists' previous clients too.

By the time you are ready to interview florists, you should have decided on the date and location of your wedding and, ideally, have chosen your wedding gown. You should have an idea of your budget and have in hand pictures of bouquets and arrangements that illustrate

FINDING A FLORIST

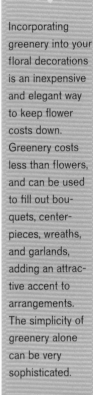

Incorporating greenery into your floral decorations is an inexpensive and elegant way to keep flower costs down. Greenery costs less than flowers, and can be used to fill out bouquets, centerpieces, wreaths, and garlands, adding an attractive accent to arrangements. The simplicity of greenery alone can be very sophisticated.

what you like and what you don't as well as fabric swatches and Polaroids of your wedding gown and attendants' gowns, and sketches, photographs, or floor plans of where your ceremony and reception will take place.

Before setting up consultations, it's helpful to narrow down your list of prospective florists by conducting a brief interview with each over the telephone. A "get acquainted" call will allow you to determine whether or not they're available on your wedding date, whether you have a rapport and will feel comfortable working with them, and what their individual style and experience are. Stay organized by keeping a record of their responses.

Opposite: *Many brides opt to use color in their floral decorations, either as an accent to white flowers or as the predominant hue.*

Above: *If you're having an outdoor wedding, be sure to look around the site for places to use greenery or flowers. Here's a good use of greenery—this heart is composed solely of lemon leaves.*

Above: *White flowers may be traditional, but they're more expensive than colored flowers. Because white flowers bruise easily, your florist will need to buy more than are called for to replace any that may be damaged from handling.*

Opposite: *Transform a generic rented chair into something special by trimming it with a garland that matches the bridal party bouquets and centerpieces. Decorating all of the reception chairs with flowers can be quite expensive, so consider reserving this special treatment for the chairs at the wedding party table only.*

Questions to Ask While Interviewing Florists over the Telephone

1. Is my wedding date available?
2. Do you charge a consultation fee?
3. What is your design style? Romantic, modern, minimal?
4. How many weddings have you produced flowers for?

Once you've determined which florists you'd like to meet with, schedule consultations with them. The consultations will allow you to get to know the florists and their work, and to discuss your ideas for your wedding. As you interview different florists, remember that you're there not only to look at the florist's portfolio of wedding arrangements but also to determine if he or she is someone you can communicate with and with whom you feel a rapport. Try to meet two or three florists, even if you feel sure you've found the right one. Prepare for the meetings by gathering magazine photos of flowers and arrangements that you like, a list of your favorite flowers, a checklist of arrangements that you think you'll need (see pages 115–117). If you have them, bring fabric swatches of your and your bridesmaids' gowns so that the florist can suggest complementary colors. Be prepared to discuss the budget as well. (Tip: Don't be shy about discussing the budget. If cost is a concern, ask about less expensive alternatives to flowers that are out of your price range. A professional florist will be able to work with any budget.) The better prepared you are, the better the meeting will go. Your ability to communicate your vision of the wedding will be a key component in

FLORAL GLOSSARY

You know what you want, but you don't know what it's called. That's the situation many brides find themselves in when it comes to flowers. Or, you don't know what you want and you need help wading through the field of floral terms to be able to explain with confidence what it is you imagine. Here's a glossary of terms to help your vocabulary blossom.

Boutonniere: A single bloom or bud (or several small buds) attached to the left lapel of the jacket. The men in your wedding party—the groom, best man, ushers, and the fathers of the bride and groom—wear these.

Buttonhole: Another name for boutonniere.

Candelabrum: A floral centerpiece created at the base, neck, or top of a multiarmed candelabrum. Such a centerpiece is usually accented with flowing greens or silk ribbons, depending on the style of the wedding.

Circlet: A floral wreath used as a headdress for the bride, bridesmaids, or flower girls that nestles at the top of the head or is placed mid-forehead.

Corsage: A single bloom or small cluster of blooms sometimes arranged against a lace or tulle doily and/or accented with ribbon. Corsages come in pin-on, wrist, and handheld styles and are typically worn by mothers and grandmothers and other special people not in the wedding party. Orchids and gardenias are popular choices.

Dais: The centerpiece at the head table where the bride and groom are seated. (The table itself also is called the dais.) This floral arrangement usually drapes over the front of the table for visual effect.

Fish Bowl: A low centerpiece style that consists of flowers clustered in a glass bowl.

Floral Foam: Special foam used in flower arrangements. The foam fits in a bouquet holder and retains water like a sponge, hydrating flowers for extended time periods.

Garden: A centerpiece featuring abstract wildflowers. The composition is generally airy and less full than other designs. Lisianthus, hollyhock, rambling roses, digitalis, herbs, and smilax are well suited to this style.

Garland: An elaborately woven rope or strand arrangement typically used to adorn pews and doorways. Garlands also can be held by two or three children and paraded down the aisle.

Hoop: Similar to a wreath and carried by bridesmaids and flower girls.

Ikebana: Japanese-style flower arrangements that are aesthetically in harmony with their surroundings.

Pomander: A bloom-covered ball suspended from a ribbon handle that is carried by brides-maids instead of a bouquet, hoop, or basket. These fragrant and unusual adornments, popular in Victorian England, are ideal for child attendants and make especially pretty keep-sakes after the wedding.

Sprig: A small cluster of blooms or a small stem of leaves or flowers taken from a larger stem or branch.

Taped and wired: A technique for arranging bouquets, boutonnieres, headpieces, and wreaths. The head of a flower is cut from the stem and attached to a wire, which is then wrapped with floral tape. Taping and/or wiring flowers makes it easier to maneuver flowers into the shapes and styles you want.

Topiary: Flowers or foliage trimmed into geometric shapes often resembling miniature trees, spheres, animals, or other forms.

Trellis: A woven wooden frame used as a screen or support for climbing plants and flowers.

Wreath: A ring of flowers or other decorative materials that can function as a centerpiece, headpiece, or door hanger.

FINDING A FLORIST

working with your florist. Working successfully with a florist usually involves some give and take (especially if, like many brides, you aren't sure exactly what you want). That's where the florist's artistry, creativity, and expertise come in. The right floral designer will not only answer your questions but listen to your concerns, come up with different options, and be sensitive to your likes and dislikes. After all, it's only by talking with you that he or she will be able to make your flowers truly personal.

If the florist has done weddings at your site before, he or she should be able to show you pictures of how they looked and tell you why certain colors, shapes, or styles work (or don't) in that space. Especially if you're a floral novice, he or she should be willing to explain what flowers go together. For example, delicate, ruffled flowers such as sweet peas don't blend well with bold sunflowers or with dramatic, angular tropical flowers such as birds of paradise. Just remember that the florist has to take in the whole picture: the month your wedding will take place, the time of day, the expected weather, the room size, lighting, your dress, market availability of different flowers, *and* your taste and budget.

Questions to Ask During the Consultation with Your Florist

1. Can you show me photographs of your work?
2. What flowers will be in season?
3. How can I make the most of my budget?
4. Have you done weddings at my ceremony and/or reception site before?
5. Will you work on my wedding flowers personally or will your staff do the work?
6. Will you be at the site on my wedding day making sure everything is in order?
7. How many weddings will you be doing on the same day as mine?
8. Do you require a deposit? Is it refundable?

Opposite: *The bride's vibrantly colored bouquet contrasts beautifully with her simple white dress, while her attendants' dresses and bouquets turn the color scheme around: bright red dresses with small bouquets where white flowers are the star.*

THE LANGUAGE OF FLOWERS

The Victorians popularized the language of flowers, whereby different meanings were attributed to different flowers and used as secret messengers of affection. The language of flowers was used by courting couples during the nineteenth century, a time when expressing certain thoughts outright would have been considered forward and improper. Thus, bouquets became imbued with secret sentiments determined by the choice and arrangement of flowers so lovers could impart messages to their dear ones through floral arrangements alone. One arrangement of flowers could propose marriage; another could accept or decline that proposal. Suitors could be encouraged or discouraged and even assignations arranged, all with the sending of the proper posy.

Although many of these floral meanings have long been forgotten, using the language of flowers can be a charming way for you to add a personal meaning to your ceremony.

Below is a sampling of flowers and their traditional meanings.

Amaryllis—Beautiful but timid; pride

Ambrosia—Love returned

Apple Blossom—Preference

Aster—Variety

Azalea—Romance

Bachelor's Button—Hope; single blessedness

Bluebell—Constancy

Buttercup—Riches

Calla Lily—Feminine beauty; modesty

Camellia—Gratitude

Camellia, Red—Loveliness

Camellia, White—Unpretending excellence

Chrysanthemum, Red—I love you

Chrysanthemum, White—Truth

Clover, White—I promise

Cowslip—Pensiveness; winning grace

Dahlia—Dignity and elegance

Daffodil—Unequaled love

Daisy, White—Innocence

Forget-Me-Not—Do not forget; true love

Four-Leaf Clover—Be mine

Fuchsia—Taste or frugality

Geranium—I prefer you; bridal favor

Geranium, Scarlet—Comfort

Heliotrope—Devotion

Hibiscus—Delicate beauty

Honeysuckle—The bond of love

Hyacinth—Constancy

Iris—A message for thee

Ivy—Friendship; fidelity

Lilac—First emotions of love

Lily of the Valley—Return of happiness

Marigold—Sacred affection

Morning Glory—Affection

Orange Blossom—Chastity; purity

Pansy—The thoughts of lovers

Peony—Bashfulness

Periwinkle, White—Pleasures of memory

Primrose—Early youth

Ranunculus—You are radiant with charms

Rose, Red—Love

Strawberry Blossom—Foresight

Sweet Basil—Good wishes

Sweet Pea—A meeting; delicate pleasures

Sweet William—Gallantry

Tulip, Red—Declaration of love

Verbena, Pink—Family union

Violet—Faithfulness, modesty

Water Lily—Purity of heart

Wisteria—I cling to thee

Zinnia—Thoughts of absent friends

The right florist will not only answer your questions but listen to your concerns, come up with different options and be sensitive to your likes and dislikes.

When you've narrowed your choices down to two or three florists, ask for a written estimate of what you've discussed. If you're having trouble making up your mind, it's acceptable to ask the florist to create a sample centerpiece or bouquet. Generally, there will be no extra charge for this service, although it's best to ask about your florist's policy first.

Once you've decided to work together, your florist will set aside your wedding date and draw up a contract. Over the next few months, you will probably meet again several times (more if the florist is providing flowers for your cake, headpieces for your bridesmaids, and other extras). At these meetings, he or she will show you centerpiece containers, finalize the placement of the ceremony flowers, and discuss other details.

Florist Contracts: What You Need to Know

Your contract or letter of agreement should nail down all the specifics you've talked about: every item, fee, date, and delivery. Getting everything spelled out ahead of time will help avoid confusion on the day of your wedding. If you've lined up your florist far in advance of your wedding, it's a good idea to call occasionally in the months before the actual event to make sure that everything is proceeding on schedule.

HERE'S WHAT YOUR CONTRACT SHOULD INCLUDE

Your name, address, and phone number and the florist's name, address, and phone number.

The name of the person with whom you've made the arrangements and the date of your appointment.

A detailed description of each service to be provided. This means the colors, types, and number of flowers in all your arrangements; the number of arrangements; and any items, such as trellises or accessories. Be sure to include an itemized list of prices.

A substitution clause in case your flowers aren't available on your wedding day. This is a list of substitute flowers in your price range that you find acceptable, so there are no unhappy surprises.

Delivery fees for all the flowers, where they should be delivered, as well as the time and date. For example, bouquets and boutonnieres may go to your home; other flowers to the ceremony and reception sites.

The total amount due, the amount of your deposit, and a payment schedule. You may be asked to put down as much as half the total. (Be sure to get a receipt.) The balance may be due anywhere from a few days to a few weeks before the wedding.

Any setup, breakdown, or overtime charges; insurance provided; rental charges (for special vases and other containers); breakage or damage policies and costs; taxes, gratuities, or other additional fees.

The last date that changes are possible as well as the florist's cancellation or refund policy if you have to cancel or if for any reason the florist is unable to provide you with what the contract calls for.

Finally, make sure you retain a copy of the original agreement, with any changes or additions signed or initialed by both you and the vendor, and put it in your wedding notebook or other safe place.

CHAPTER 10

Bouquets

Your bridal bouquet is one of the most important floral elements of your wedding. Year after year, women all over the world walk down the aisle carrying their own choice of carefully selected, artfully assembled flowers. So strongly ingrained is the tradition of the bridal bouquet that even the woman who marries in jeans and T-shirt will still be carrying some kind of flowers. More so than a wedding gown, it's the bouquet that makes her a bride.

Throughout history, brides have carried bouquets to the altar, one of the many wedding rituals that have been associated with flowers. In some early cultures, it was the custom for brides to carry flowers mixed with strong herbs (such as garlic or chives) to ward off evil spirits and prevent bad luck. Sprinkling flower petals in the bride's path as she walks down the aisle originated from the idea of protecting her from evil spirits who dwell below ground.

It was the Victorians, in particular, who gave us many of the wedding traditions still practiced today, especially those that involve flowers. Victorian brides were the

first to marry in white and as noted earlier, it was Victorian lovers who, during courtship, popularized the romantic language of flowers. A bridal bouquet made only from pure white flowers was yet another Victorian custom, one that flourished throughout the twentieth century and is still popular today. So, too, was the creation of a good luck bell (or horseshoe or other lucky symbol) also made entirely of white flowers. These were traditionally suspended over the spot where the bride and groom would stand together at the altar.

Wedding bouquets range from the sublimely simple to the lushly elegant. The most traditional are composed of all white or near-white flowers. This incredibly beautiful and popular look suits any kind of wedding, formal or informal alike. White roses, stephanotis, or all-white lilies of the valley for example, combined with some green foliage, have a timeless elegance. Even common white baby's breath can look starry and spectacular when carried on its own, worn with a simple gown and headpiece. (Tip: It's

Page 158: Red, purple, yellow, and orange come together to create this sumptuous bouquet. The vivid palette was inspired by the bride's embroidered wedding shoes.

Opposite: Sprays of buds and berries in rich red and cranberry tones combined with roses add opulence to a winter wedding.

Left, above: This elegant presentation, or pageant, bouquet consists of white roses with a lovely mix of greenery to round out the arrangement.

Left, below: By including sprigs of herbs, ivy, and ferns, this bouquet is filled with botanical symbols of marital health and happiness. Herbs have played a role in weddings throughout history, representing a variety of good wishes for the bride and groom.

Opposite: *This formal bouquet is composed of roses, calla lilies, and gardenias surrounded by dark green leaves. Gardenias have an exquisite fragrance, but are delicate and bruise easily.*

Right: *The tissue-pink Oceana roses in this bride's nosegay perfectly complement the pale pink silk rosettes on her gown. The sheer pink ribbon adds a flourish of color.*

Below: *A sumptuous bouquet of lavender roses. In the Victorian language of flowers, lavender roses symbolize enchantment.*

also inexpensive, long-lasting, and dries beautifully.) Other popular white bridal flowers are ranunculus, gardenias, calla lilies, orchids, hydrangeas, freesia, and Madonna lilies.

Bouquets that contrast different floral shapes, colors, and textures also are popular, such as traditional roses with peonies, hydrangea, and sweet peas. Flowers in offbeat or unusual colors such as mango, fuchsia, and purple can be especially appealing at casual weddings, while a bride who marries in a beachside ceremony might carry a bouquet adorned with tiny starfish or sea shells. Are you intrigued by the idea of adding herbs to your bouquet? Try a combination of geranium leaves, lemon thyme, basil, lavender, and mint.

The style and flowers chosen for the bride's bouquet set the theme for all the personal flowers for your wedding. Usually it's only after the bridal bouquet has been chosen that flowers are selected for the rest of the wedding party, so that they complement but don't overshadow the bridal bouquet in style, flower selection, and color.

Bouquet Shapes

Bouquets come in many different shapes. Here's a list of classic bouquet shapes for the bride and other members of the bridal party.

POSY

Smaller than nosegays but similar in design, posies have an old-fashioned feel. They work best with smaller blooms, although a few large flowers, such as peonies, can make a statement. Posies are often chosen for bridesmaids or flowers girls. Here, yellow roses and anemones make up this bride's charming posy.

BIEDERMEIER

Also called a ring bouquet, Biedermeier bouquets are a more formal variation of the round bouquet. They are composed of tightly arranged concentric circles of various multicolored flowers. The blooms are wired into a holder, with one flower variety per ring. This Biedermeier is designed with creamy tulips in the center, surrounded by muscari, with ivory roses forming the outside ring.

POMANDER

A ball of flowers suspended from the wrist by a decorative ribbon handle. A sweet alternative for junior bridesmaids and flower girls.

HAND-TIED

Bouquets arranged and held in the hand with the body of the flowers facing upward as if they had been picked fresh from the garden. The stems are wrapped with ribbon and may include a bow accent. This one features roses, hyacinths, lilies of the valley, and other small white blooms.

PRESENTATION (OR SHEAF)

A collection of long-stemmed flowers held in the crook of the arm, typically tied together with ribbons. This presentation bouquet composed of long-stemmed roses tied with a lavender ribbon makes a simple yet elegant bridal bouquet.

ROUND

Similar in style to a nosegay but larger, the round bouquet is ideal for any style of wedding. Here, an abundance of white roses punctuated with a few green leaves make up a classic round bouquet.

CASCADE (OR SHOWER)

A luxurious and formal style, cascades have a waterfall-like spill of blooms, often composed of ivy and long-stemmed flowers, wired to flow (or cascade) over the bride's hands. Light, graceful flowers work best in cascades. This cascade bouquet is designed with white roses and stephanotis.

NOSEGAY

Small, simple, circular bouquets composed of densely packed round flowers, greenery, and occasionally herbs. A versatile shape, nosegays are wired together and anchored in bouquet holders, or tied together. A typical small nosegay might include baby rosebuds, violets, and bachelor's buttons; a larger, looser one might be composed of narcissus and orchids, or old-fashioned roses, such as the nosegay shown here.

HOW TO HOLD YOUR BOUQUET

Before the big day, take time to practice walking while holding your bouquet properly (use a stand-in, such as a book, or buy some flowers to practice with) so that you best feature both the bouquet and your dress as you walk down the aisle. Stand in front of a mirror to check your form; be sure that you're not obscuring your dress or holding the bouquet too low (in which case no one will see your beautiful flowers). If you'll be escorted down the aisle by another person (or two people), practice linking arms with them while holding your bouquet.

Handheld Bouquet: Hold your wrists just above your hipbones and use both hands to hold the stems of the bouquet in front of your belly button. Point your elbows out a little bit, to reveal the curve of your waist and show off your dress.

Presentation Bouquet: Rest the bouquet on the lower part of your arm; don't hold it too closely or you'll risk crushing it.

Other Bouquet Shapes

Composite: A bouquet that uses petals from one or several flowers creating the illusion of a single, oversized bloom.

Spray Bouquet: A triangular-shaped cluster of flowers.

Tussy Mussy: From the Victorian era, a tussy mussy is a posy carried in a small, metallic (often silver or silver-plated) ornamental holder.

Bouquet Tips

Here are a few tips to keep in mind when considering bouquet shapes and styles.

Your bridal bouquet is an accessory that should enhance but not overshadow your gown. Remember to bring a swatch of your wedding gown fabric with you when you choose your bouquet, along with a sketch or photograph of the gown itself.

Add sentimental meaning to your wedding and honor your mother by carrying a bouquet made up of the same flowers she carried (or your grandmother carried). And remember to write down what they are so your own daughter can continue the tradition. (By the way, make a copy of that list for your husband. That way, he can send you the same bouquet on your first anniversary, and every year thereafter!)

Keep proportion—yours and your gown's—in mind when choosing the bouquet style you want. Taller brides can carry larger, cascading bouquets; if you're small, you'll look more natural with a smaller bouquet.

If there's an embellishment on your gown that you want to be seen, discuss it with your florist and ask him or her to recommend a suitable bouquet style.

The bigger, fuller, and more formal your dress, the bigger, fuller and more formal your bouquet should be.

Be sure that your bouquet is easy to carry—neither too heavy nor too cumbersome. You want to walk down the aisle with grace and ease, and not worry about fussing with or handling your flowers.

Opposite: *To complement the bride's wedding gown, the floral designer created a nosegay of soft, fully open pink and lavender roses spiked with maroon buds.*

Left: *Creamy white roses mixed with white and lavender hydrangeas comprise this traditional round bouquet.*

Don't overlook the importance of greenery and foliage in your bouquet. Lacy ferns, ivy, and other greens can provide a wealth of textures and even different colors (like soft brown-greens, deep green, and rich bronze shades, or the silvery tones of Dusty Miller).

Keep the mood of your bouquet in harmony with the formality of the affair. A bouquet of fresh green wheat and wildflowers suits a country wedding, not a white-tie reception.

If you're carrying lilies, be sure your florist removes the stamens to prevent pollen from staining your dress.

CHAPTER II

Flowers for the Wedding Party

Traditionally, flowers for the wedding party include bouquets for the bridesmaids and maid and matron of honor, a basket of flowers for the flower girl, corsages for the mothers of the bride and groom, and boutonnieres for all the men—the groom,

the fathers, the best man, the ushers, and even the ring bearer. Flowers can be ordered for other specials guests as well, such as stepparents, grandparents, and godparents.

Bridesmaids, Mothers, and Flower Girls

Bouquets for the women in the bridal party take their cue from the bride's bouquet. Often, they're somewhat smaller but echo her bouquet in the choice of flowers, shape, colors, or other elements. The flowers for the maid or matron of honor usually reflect those of the maids but are also distinctive: If the bridesmaids are carrying pink roses, for example, the maid of honor might carry roses in multi-colored shades of pink, from petal pale to rich scarlet, or variegated roses in deep pink and white.

But bouquets aren't the only flower option. Some brides select wicker flower baskets for their attendants, densely packed with flowers (especially pretty in spring or summer), or woodland-style baskets nested with moss and herbs. Baskets should be light, easy to carry (especially important for the flower girl), able to stand firmly without toppling, and easily transportable. Note: While flower girls traditionally strew rose or other flower petals in the bride's path during the

Page 172: Red is the signature element in this bride's color scheme. Red is considered a deeply romantic color, and takes on special significance around holidays like Valentine's Day and Christmas. A close-up photograph of the bride's bouquet can be seen on page 158.

Opposite: The difference between the bride's bouquet and the bridesmaids' bouquets can be subtle. For this wedding, the bride's bouquet consisted of pale pink roses while the bridesmaids' posies featured darker-toned tea-colored roses.

Above: Lacy ferns and silvery Dusty Miller add a wealth of textures and colors to these two attendants' bouquets of pink snowberries and lavender roses.

Below: Bouquets for the bridesmaids take their cue from the bride's. Although smaller, they often include similar flowers, colors or other related elements.

processional, another option is to have your flower girl give a single rose to every guest sitting along the aisle.

For weddings with a period or rustic theme, bridesmaids may carry a Shakespearean-style garland of fresh flowers, and for weddings with an Elizabethan or Victorian flavor, why not consider floral pomanders for your attendants?

Floral hoops are a charming option for a young bridesmaid, flower girl, or page boy. (Hoops are often easier for children to carry than a basket.) To complement a floral hoop, flower girls and junior bridesmaids generally wear in their hair a matching flower circlet, such as an ivy vine loosely wrapped

Opposite: *Like a wedding ring, a floral circlet is a circle without beginning or end. To crown a veil, what could be prettier than this classic circlet of silken roses?*

Above: *Traditionally suspended over the spot where the bride and groom would stand together at the altar, a horseshoe made entirely of white flowers was meant to bring the couple good luck in their life together. In a modern take on the custom, this flower girl carried the horseshoe down the aisle.*

Right: *Long-stemmed pink sweet peas and paperwhites overflow from this flower girl's basket.*

WEARING FLOWERS IN YOUR HAIR

Every bride aspires to be the epitome of romance on this, her most romantic day, and nothing suggests romance as much as bedecking your hair with flowers. At the same time, wilted or browning flowers strewn throughout your hair are certainly less than lovely. So what can you do to keep the flowers you choose for your hair fresh and beautifully blooming?

If you plan to wear a headpiece adorned with flowers, such as a floral crown or a floral tiara attached to the veil (or even used without a veil), the best option is to have two headpieces, one for the ceremony and pictures, another for the reception. This will ensure that the flowers stay fresh looking.

The same holds true of individual flowers woven into your coiffure. Flowers may be braided, pinned, or woven into the hair, and most florists are happy to provide a second set of flowers to reweave into the hair before the reception. (Hairstylists generally take care to arrange the flowers so they are easy to remove and replace.)

Flowers are usually wired and then taped with florist tape to make them easier to handle, although some hairstylists prefer to work with flowers in their natural state. Many prefer using smaller blooms, as they tend to last longer and it's easier to work the stems into the hair. Stephanotis, a delicate, white, star-shaped flower that adds an air of innocence and elegance, is a bridal favorite, as are other smaller, hardy flowers such as narcissus, daisies, smaller varieties of orchids, and spray roses or miniature roses.

Be sure to discuss with your florist the flowers you are considering for your hair; he or she is a good resource as to what types of flowers make the best hair accessories.

Getting the flowers from your florist also will ensure that they match or complement your bouquet. Blooms such as jasmine, bulb flowers such as tulips or daffodils, and large flowers tend to wilt faster, so keep that in mind and make sure to have duplicates.

If you are planning to have a stylist do your hair, it's a good idea to do a practice run before the wedding. That way you can ensure that the style is to your liking and that you can move around, dance, etc., without the flowers falling out, as well as learn how to replace them easily if need be. Because it's always a bit disheartening to see a bedraggled bride, on the day of the wedding the bride's hair is usually done last so she looks as fresh as possible, and the flowers do too.

Another important factor to keep in mind before you put flowers in your hair: Make sure that you and your groom both find their fragrance pleasing.

Floral headpieces to consider:

Circlet—A floral wreath that nestles on top of your head or at mid-forehead.

Coronet—A floral wreath that rests high on the crown of your head.

Garden Hat—A crownless hat trimmed with flowers and ribbons.

Hair Bow—Usually made of satin or lace and positioned at the back of the head, often flower trimmed.

Headband—A raised hair band, often decorated and ornamented with flowers.

Tiara—A type of headpiece made up of fresh or silk flowers, or a combination of both, typically held together with wire. (A fresh one will usually last a full day out of water.)

SILK FLOWERS
Another option for floral headpieces is to use silk flowers; these, of course, always look fresh (and may even be a better choice for little girls since children tend to be hard on things anyway). Gaining popularity among brides, silk flowers look extremely real, don't wilt, can become keep-sakes, and most of the time are less expensive than fresh flowers. In terms of price, high-quality silks are equivalent to medium- to low-priced fresh flowers, whereas medium- to low-quality silks are less expensive than fresh.

on a framework of birch twigs with flowers and berries attached. Flower girls can also wear a headband with rosebuds or pansies and lily of the valley attached and, instead of conventional flower baskets, carry miniature watering cans filled with lilies, irises, and pansies.

In addition to those they carry, bridesmaids often wear their flowers, sometimes head to toe: in the crown of a wide-brimmed straw hat, attached to a silk ribbon worn

Far left: *Using silk flowers is becoming an increasingly popular choice. They are a terrific option for your hair, because they look fresh all day.*

Near left: *Floral crowns are perennial favorites for flower girls. This young flower girl wears a wreath of creamy roses and rosemary.*

around the neck (instead of a locket or pearls), even as trim on their shoes (think of
tiny rosebuds or miniature silk bachelor's buttons). Muffs trimmed in flowers or
made entirely of flowers are pretty at winter weddings, and flower purses created by
your florist are a charming and increasingly popular choice often favored by mothers
of the bride and grooms who don't care for corsages. Other options for mothers of the
bride and groom include small nosegays or flowers worn in their hair or on a headpiece, or a silk-flower ornament studded with gold or crystal beading. If a traditional,
sweet-smelling corsage (usually an orchid) is worn, it's generally pinned above the left

Opposite: *If the mothers
of the bride and groom
do not want to wear a
corsage, another option
is to have them carry a
small nosegay.*

Above: *Small posies are
perfect for small hands.
This one is composed of
lilies of the valley.*

breast on a suit or covered dress, on the shoulder strap of a bare dress, attached to an evening bag or purse, or worn as a wristlet.

Boutonnieres

Boutonnieres, gallantly pinned to the left lapel of all the men in your wedding party, are worn at informal daytime weddings and formal nighttime affairs alike. Also called buttonholes, these typically are single flowers (such as white or red roses), although less conventional choices include two or three rosebuds, a sprig of freesia, or a few buds of stephanotis with a bit of ivy. Indeed, nowadays, anything goes: a sprig of white lilac, tiny roses mixed with hyacinth . . .

One old-time custom calls for the bride to pluck a flower from her bouquet and tenderly pin it to the groom's left lapel before the ceremony. Although this is seldom

Far right and near right: Two classic boutonnieres. The groom's boutonniere usually reflects the flowers in the bridal bouquet and should be slightly different from those of the groomsmen in the wedding party.

observed today (most brides are too nervous), the groom's boutonniere is frequently composed of one or two of the same flowers as in the bride's bouquet and is often slightly different in appearance from those of the other men in the wedding party. Tip: If you are having your wedding pictures taken before the ceremony, ask your florist for a second boutonniere, so your groom can replace the one that may have wilted or become lackluster after greeting everyone and kissing them hello. Also, if the men in the wedding party are to wear breast-pocket handkerchiefs, boutonnieres are not worn.

Above: *A small posy of yellow roses. A yellow rose means friendship in the language of flowers.*

Left: *If the family pet will be attending the wedding, he or she can also wear flowers! Here, the bride's bull mastiff completed the bridal party, sporting a garland of orchids and ivy. The orchids matched those used throughout the wedding site.*

CHAPTER 12

Flowers for the Ceremony and Reception

Decorating your ceremony site with flowers adds to the beauty and festive nature of the occasion, enhancing the sense of joy for you, your groom, and your guests. But no two places are alike—ceremony venues range from houses of worship, hotels, and living rooms to galleries, lofts, parks, gardens, and more—and they don't all have the same policies on the use of floral decorations. Some venues may not permit additional flowers, floral altar decorations, or other adornments at all. So be sure that you or your florist obtain any permissions required.

Below are ideas on how to use flowers to make the site of your ceremony special.

Colorful floral wreaths or garlands on doors create an immediate sense of welcome for arriving guests. Particularly effective are seasonal touches: a wreath of gilded pinecones and berries in winter; branches of flowering forsythia, dogwood, or

Page 184: *A simple floral accent, hydrangeas festoon the peaked roof over the entrance to this church.*

Opposite and right: *A handsome barn was the site of this reception. The floral decorations on the exterior and interior were very simple—the colors and flower varieties are the same as those in the bride's bouquet—and were accented by small twinkling lights decorating the ceiling and posts in the barn.*

cherry blossoms in spring; a sheaf of wheat for good luck in late summer or fall. Inside, enliven simple spaces with floral archways or bowers along the aisle, and matching floral arrangements on either side. Windowsills, fonts, lecterns, choir stalls, and pillars all provide opportunities for floral display.

Right: *Pew decorations composed of small bouquets of orchids.*

Far right: *Flower petals ready to hand out to guests for tossing.*

In a large church or synagogue, consider a single, dramatic floral arrangement at the altar or, alternatively, two matching arrangements on either side of the aisle. The grander the setting, the larger and more dramatic the flowers should be; opt for long-stemmed blooms rather than small, short-stemmed blossoms, which tend to get visually lost in a large space.

Pew and chair decorations need to be carefully thought out so they don't obstruct the aisle in any way. Steer clear of anything that will block the view of the bridal procession, interfere with the flow of the bride's train, or impede the procession's

FLOWERS FOR THE CEREMONY AND RECEPTION

walk down the aisle. If there is room, consider baskets or pots filled with flowers at the ends of the pews, or hang small garlands at the ends, to earmark those pews set aside for family members.

In putting together an at-home wedding, be as lavish with flowers as your budget permits. Hang a floral wreath on the door. Place flowers in the hallway, on stairway landings, entwined in chandeliers, on the fireplace mantel, side tables, and even in the bathrooms where guests go to freshen up. Outside, porch railings and pillars are ideal places for ivy vines and other greenery, and hanging baskets overflowing with flowers always add a festive touch.

After the ceremony, to shower the bride and groom with flower petals (instead of rice or birdseed), place petals near the doors so guests can easily take a handful as they exit. Or fill individual glassine envelopes or cones with petals and pass them around in big baskets so guests will have something to hold the petals in before tossing.

Above: For an at-home wedding, dress up chairs with a swathe of pure-white blossoms tied with pale blue ribbon.

Reception Flowers and Table Settings

When your guests finally walk into your reception area—be it at home or at a country club, reception hall, hotel, or some other location—you'll want quite simply to take their breath away. That's where all the weeks and months of planning and designing your flowers come in. For the most part, it's the reception flowers that truly set the mood and create the festive atmosphere for the celebration of your life.

Long before the arrival of your wedding date, your florist will have already visited the reception site (probably several times). Will pedestals or columns be needed? Are there balconies, archways, or other interesting architectural features that could be highlighted with flowers and greenery? The florist needs to decide beforehand where the flower arrangements are going to go before he or she decides to make them tall or wide, round or full. And where to slip in the touches—the fresh lemon leaves arranged in the shape of a heart and hung like a wreath on the entry door or a heart-shaped basket packed with tiny blossoms for the place-card table—that make your wedding unique.

Opposite: *A blend of simplicity and sophistication: lush bouquets in fiery red and orange hues that are low enough for easy conversation.*

Left: *Small clay pots surrounding a white vase filled with white flowers make a charming centerpiece. The clay pots could also be used as favors for your guests.*

As brides have become more knowledgeable about flowers, so wedding center-pieces and table settings are being designed with more individual flair, combining tradition with invention. So look beyond the usual bridal clichés to add a touch of surprise, glamour, or whimsy to your celebration. It could be as simple as placing sparkly little votive lights encircled by tiny flowers at each place setting. Or setting small bunches of lily of the valley, grape hyacinth, or violets in tiny bottles on a mantel. One designer delights in using different types of containers on each table—unmatched teacups, milk-glass pitchers, terra-cotta urns, silver canisters, or other unconventional objects—each holding a different type of flower, for what she calls "an at-home, residential look."

Seasonal accents can add special significance: a cornucopia of ferns, moss, pinecones, gourds, and harvest leaves together with rich-toned flowers in amber, burgundy, and russet tones for fall; winter's forest evergreens mixed with lush garnet roses; or a sparkling "wonderland" of all-white flowers paired with shimmery crystal beads in gleaming silver canisters. For spring and summer, how about combining oranges, lemons, and other fruits in arrangements with flowering branches of cherry, apple, or quince?

Below are some guidelines along with trends and tips to what's new and noteworthy:

Height: Floral arrangements should be either very high or quite low, so your guests can see each other and make conversation across the table. For rooms with high ceilings or big spaces, consider tall glass cylinders filled halfway with polished stones and holding sweeping floral branches. Or an elegant wrought-iron candelabrum with hanging votives and strewn petals at its base. For a low centerpiece, try a cluster of five or six small arrangements grouped together that guests can then take away as

Opposite: Victorian candelabrum and towering vases adorn the dinner tables on the tented lawn at this reception. The height of each arrangement adds a dramatic touch to this sumptuous display, yet allow guests to converse with ease. All-white flowers set off with glossy greenery are massed at the candelabra bases for interest at eye level.

FLOWERS FOR THE CEREMONY AND RECEPTION

If you're creating your own center-pieces, keep in mind the florists' rule of thumb: The vase or con-tainer should be one-half to one-third the size of the total arrange-ment (e.g., three-foot delphiniums or gladiolus need a twelve- to eighteen-inch vase).

favors. If you're not sure about what you've chosen, ask your florist to make up a sample and place it on the table to see if you like it.

A Tisket, a Tasket: Baskets, a perennial wedding favorite, are economical and available in countless graceful shapes. You can fill them with flowers—informal blooms such as tulips, daisies, and sweet peas are good choices for most baskets—or line them with a linen napkin and fill them with bread. Bread baskets evoke a coun-try or harvest theme and give guests something to eat as soon as they are seated. Another option in keeping with a country or harvest theme is to fill baskets with lemons, apples, peaches, or nectarines—fruits with strong colors.

Light: Tall candelabrum centerpieces, while dramatic and beautiful, require a minimal number of flowers; they need just a few bits of greenery and blossoms around the base and some flowers entwined around the branches. Candles of all sizes and heights interspersed among vases of flowers create a look that's elegant and romantic.

Opposite: Sunflowers are a terrific choice for a summer wedding. The square metal buckets add a casual air to the table decorations and work perfectly with the checkered yellow table cloths and napkins.

Left: A centerpiece composed of multicol-ored roses in shades of coral-rose, peach, ivory, and pink tops a glass bowl filled with seashells—perfect for a summer wedding by the seashore. Seashells also are strewn on the table and used as napkin rings.

Opposite: *The elegance of a monochromatic and formal table is enhanced with bunches of white blooms, including a single gardenia in a silver cup.*

Right: *A simple yet chic table setting composed of a single spray of orchids and three votive candles. The camera allows guests to take their own candid shots of the reception.*

Far right: *There are myriad ways to add a special floral touch to your reception, such as this single rose adorning a caterer's tray.*

Creative Containers: Unusual containers are increasingly popular (think pewter, silver plate, faux mother-of-pearl, or porcelain).

Mix It Up: Whimsical arrangements featuring berries, grasses, and flowers, and luscious fruits, such as blueberries, champagne grapes, figs, and even vegetables, add charm and make out-of-the-ordinary centerpieces.

Keep It Simple . . . Again: Lots of brides want simpler, smaller centerpieces. Consider floating candles amid floating flowers; or a single candle in the center of each table with rose petals sprinkled around the base.

Special Touches: Consider a different centerpiece for the bride and groom's own table; decorating the bride and groom's chairs with twisted vines, flowers, and foliage; flower ice cubes at the bar (place an edible blossom in each compartment of an ice tray, add water, and freeze; in summer, try nasturtium or mint); and floral-adorned

menus for guests (slip menus into napkins, fold, tie with a ribbon, and tuck a fresh flower into the bow).

Favorite Flowers: Exotic orchids are still many a bride's dream flower, especially the more unusual varieties. Lush, romantic hydrangeas come in a range of colors (blue, lavender, pinks, and pale greens) and elegant dahlias (clean, crisp) are showing up at fashionable weddings, as are humble carnations—a great choice for brides on a budget. In offbeat colors such as lime green or hot pink, masses of spicy little carnations tightly packed into a centerpiece look colorful, fresh, and very attractive.

Opposite: *Burgundy peonies and tulips anchor this exuberant and sophisticated arrangement.*

Above, left: *Roses, green hydrangea, and lemon leaves in silver cups adorn this bar set up at an outdoor wedding.*

Above, right: *A delicate flourish at the table— soft pink table linens are caught up with sweet peas and sprigs of lilac and tied with ivy.*

Decorating the Wedding Cake and Cake Table

Today, while still elaborately decorated, wedding cakes are more often than not crowned with fresh flowers. Fresh flowers also often decorate cake tables too.

Flowers for your wedding cake are the result of collaboration between you, your baker, and your florist. At the very least, your baker will need to give the top tier diameter measurement to your florist (usually six to eight inches). The florist then covers a plastic dish with greenery and flowers to set on top (almost like a corsage but without the pin!) and provides petals to sprinkle on and around the cake. Other options are more elaborate, taking into consideration the color of the icing, the flavor of the cake, or the wedding theme. Tiered cakes with flowers in between the tiers can also be created, with anything from blue hydrangeas to red roses—anything goes—but beware of poisonous flowers such as foxgloves or poinsettias. Consult with your florist to see which flowers are edible or nonpoisonous. In addition, it is essential that you make sure that the flowers for your cake haven't been sprayed with insecticides or other toxic materials.

Your baker must deliver the cake early enough so that the florist can decorate it properly (it can take an hour or more to decorate a large cake). Note: Even though flowers and greenery are carefully washed before being placed on the cake, all florists and bakers caution that they still should *never* be eaten.

Because the bride and groom are usually photographed with the wedding cake, the table is also often decorated. Similar decorations can be designed for the guestbook table and any other special locations at the reception.

Opposite: *Remember that the wedding cake will be one of the most photographed elements of the reception. Why not make it picture perfect? Here, an array of roses, lilies, and stephanotis mixed with greenery complete the romantic look of this cake.*

Above: *A few hydrangea blooms dress up this traditional white wedding cake perfectly.*

CHAPTER 13

Your Wedding Day

After months of careful preparation, the big day has arrived! In the morning, confirm with your florist when and where your flowers will arrive, and how they'll be distributed among the bridal party. Where will your wedding pictures be taken? Your florist should arrive at the site around the same time as the photographer, since you'll want to have the bouquets, boutonnieres, and corsages ready for all your photographs. Be sure to check the delivery carefully to ensure that the right flowers have been delivered and that they're in good condition. Your florist should inspect the flowers as well as soon as possible and remove any bruised or damaged petals. Have a friend or family member—someone who knows all the members of the bridal party—help the florist distribute the bridesmaids' bouquets, corsages, and boutonnieres.

Flower Delivery

On the big day, the following schedule should be followed:

2 to 3 Hours Before the Ceremony: Your reception flowers should be delivered to the reception venue for setup. (Don't forget to tip the delivery people; ask a family member or one of the bridal party members to handle this for you.)

1 to 2 Hours Before the Ceremony: The flowers should be delivered to the church or other ceremony location for setup. Make sure everyone has their bouquet, boutonniere, or corsage, and, if the flower girls and ring bearer need flowers that they have theirs, too. Bridesmaids' bouquets can be handed out just before they walk down the aisle, unless photos are being taken before the ceremony.

At the Ceremony: After greeting your fiancé at the altar, hand your bouquet to your maid of honor. She should return it to you when you head back down the aisle.

At the Reception: Traditionally, the bride's bouquet is placed on the cake table. However, the bouquet may be displayed anywhere: on the cake table; the gift, guest-book, or place-card table; or even in a vase on the head table.

Page 202: The happy day has arrived!

Above: According to tradition, the bride's bouquet is placed on the cake table. This is a nice way to decorate the cake table, and it also gives guests the opportunity to admire your bouquet close-up.

Preserving the Bride's Bouquet

Because so much thought goes into selecting a bridal bouquet, many brides choose not to toss it (or to toss a duplicate, called a "tossing bouquet") but prefer instead to preserve it as a precious romantic keepsake.

There are a number of ways to preserve fresh flowers, and it's best to consult with your florist to determine the best method for preserving the particular flowers you have chosen (he or she may be able to do it for you). Keep in mind that most flowers will darken: white flowers turn cream or ivory, and others turn brown. Also, some methods of flower preservation last longer than others; dried flowers not treated with a preserving agent, for example, may only last a few months.

If you choose to preserve your bouquet professionally, make the arrangements before the event so the process can begin as soon as possible after the celebrations—who wants to preserve a half-dead bouquet? The same applies if you're going to do it yourself: Don't wait too long. It's for this reason that some brides have the florist deliver a duplicate bouquet for preservation purposes, after they return from the honeymoon.

To keep your bouquet truest to its original form, freeze-drying is the most faithful method thus far. It takes twelve to fourteen days to complete the process and is a bit pricey ($165 to $600), but there's really no way to do it on your own. Your flowers are first treated with a

---

THE BOUQUET TOSS

Following the reception, many brides still happily participate in the bouquet toss, flinging their bouquets (or a duplicate made especially for the ritual) into a crowd of single female well-wishers, all of whom vie for the honor of catching it, thereby becoming (or so says tradition), the next woman to marry.* The origin of the custom goes back to the second half of the nineteenth century, when brides dismantled their bouquets after the wedding and presented a flower to each bridesmaid. This practice evolved into bridal bouquets actually being fashioned from numerous smaller bouquets held together with ribbons that were untied and the posies distributed to the bride's attendants. The lucky maid who received the one with a golden ring inside was heralded as the next bride-to-be.

Even though it's a long-standing tradition, some brides and their friends find the bouquet toss ritual a bit embarrassing. So they may opt to give their bouquet to someone special. If you choose to do the same, and your bouquet contains ivy, why not cut off a snippet and plant it in an ornamental pot or in your garden as a remembrance all your married days.

*The bouquet toss was also said to serve as a distraction for wedding guests, as the commotion allowed the bride and groom to "steal away" on their wedding trip without being followed.

**KEEPING
YOUR FLOWERS
FRESH**

To ensure that
your bouquets
stay as fresh as
possible before
the ceremony,
keep them out of
direct sunlight,
away from heat
and humidity, and
away from cold
drafts. Hand-tied
bouquets can be
kept in glasses
of water right
up until the last
moment, but
be sure to dry
them off so the
water doesn't
stain your wed-
ding gown or
the bridesmaids'
dresses.

chemical to prevent bubbles from forming and to preserve their color, then flash frozen in a special machine that draws out the moisture. Afterward, a polymer spray is applied to increase their longevity. Although the blooms are fragile, there is gener- ally minimal shrinkage as the quick drying crystallizes the blossoms, so they remain almost lifelike. Colors tend to fade slightly as the flowers age. According to experts, orchids, daisies, Asiatic lilies, and bouvardia are the least suited to this method.

Air-drying is another popular choice, and the best way to do this is to take your bouquet apart and dry the flowers separately. Tie a cotton string around the stem of each flower and hang it upside down from the ceiling in a warm, dark room. When dried (one to three weeks, depending on the type of flower), coat with a finishing spray (such as Krylon); otherwise the flowers will be too brittle. Because of the brit- tle nature of air-dried flowers, putting the bouquet back together is the most difficult part. Still, it's best not to try to hang your entire bouquet. Not only will it take a very long time to dry, but it may dry unevenly (the outer flowers drying more quickly, the inner ones staying moist); and brightly colored flowers can stain lighter ones. Other risks: Flowers may start to decompose, and if you live in an area where the humidity is high, mold can grow on the flowers.

For dehydrated flowers, air circulation is also used. It is best to purchase a dehydrator ($100 to $200 at outdoor or camping shops or from specialty cooking catalogs) for this method. Since most dehydrators are too small for large or even medium-size bouquets, experts recommend that you dehydrate each flower individually. Dehydrating is a faster method of preservation than air-drying, but you must remember to turn the flowers often so they don't get flattened on one side. If you choose to frame the bouquet in a deep shadowbox frame, this method is perfect.

For quicker results, try microwave drying. Place a layer of silica gel (available in most craft stores) in a microwave-safe glass dish, and set the timer for one minute. The silica gel will turn blue. Place the flowers on top, then add another layer of silica gel to cover the flowers completely. Microwave for one to three minutes (varies with microwave), remove the dish, and let the flowers sit for twenty to thirty minutes. Microwave drying is best for flowers with many petals and "deep forms," such as marigolds, roses, carnations, and zinnias (steer clear of flowers with thin, delicate petals or hairy, sticky surfaces). When done, the flowers should be completely dry, but if not,

apply another layer of silica gel and let them sit for five to ten additional minutes.

Besides silica gel, other desiccants can be used to dry the flowers in your bouquet, including alum or borax mixed with cornmeal (one part to two parts, respectively). To draw the moisture out of flowers with this method, spread the drying agent you've chosen in a container, and place the flowers on the agent. Daisies and other blossoms with a single row of petals should be placed bloom side down on the mixture, whereas flowers with long stalks, such as delphiniums, should be placed sideways and multipetal blooms, such as roses, can be upright. Then, add more of the drying agent over the flowers and store in a cool, dark place. Drying times vary, depending on the agent, but generally about a week will do it. When the flowers are completely dry, brush them with a soft paintbrush or makeup brush to remove any remaining mixture.

Although glycerin does not work well with most flowers, it does work beautifully on greenery and baby's breath. Here's how: Add glycerin to hot tap water in a vase or other container, one part to two parts, respectively. Then smash the stem of whatever foliage you are drying and place it in the mixture for up to three weeks. The

Above: Special touches marked this romantic garden wedding, including a floral collar for a winsome cat sculpture.

mixture can be reused, and the material you've preserved should be stored in a cool, dry place. This is one method that does not cause the foliage to become brittle.

For pressed flowers, your best bet is to use a simple flower press, which can be purchased in a craft store or easily made at home. (To make a press, take two pieces of wood and with a screw and bolt, fasten at each corner. Use pliers to tighten and loosen the bolts as needed.) A couple of very large, heavy books can be used as well.

When laying out the flowers, make sure to use paper (blotting paper or even typing paper works well) between the layers of flowers to absorb moisture and any stains that the flowers may produce.

Place the paper between each layer so flowers don't touch the ones above or below. The flowers are essentially flattened but will retain some shape and, occasionally, the impression of the flower being pressed above or below it. Let them sit for five to six weeks—a longer drying process ensures better color retention, but most flowers will be darkened, muted, or browned.

To simply preserve the essence of the bouquet, potpourri is a lovely option. The best way to dry the leaves and petals of the flowers is to use a dehydrator, although you can also use the air-dry method, placing them in a flat basket or on a screen. Separate the petals and leaves, then cover with cheesecloth to protect them from dust and dirt and let them sit until dry. Add a few drops of essential oil like lavender or lemon balm, and mix. Place in a sealed glass jar and shake occasionally to mature scent. It's a practical and useful way to keep your bouquet around for years to come.

> If you choose to preserve your bouquet professionally, make the arrangements before the event so the process can begin as soon as possible after the celebrations—who wants to preserve a half-dead bouquet?

Acknowledgments

We would like to gratefully acknowledge all those whose knowledge, editorial assistance, and photographs have contributed to this book. Their input has been invaluable, and we thank them:

Christa Weber, AKL Studio, NYC; Tom and Dennis at Ariston Florists, NYC; Francis De La Hoz, hairstylist, Devachan Salon, NYC; Kathy Reid at Heller & Reid Bridal Bouquet Preservation, Richardson, Texas; Monica at Beers Flower Shop, Ridgewood, NJ; Inna at City Blossoms, NYC; Anthony Rodriguez at Fellan Florist, NYC; the wedding consultants at Marcy Blum Associates, NYC; Wendy Kraus at Bloom, NYC; Special Events Consultant Susan Chagnon, NYC; Stuart Brownstein at Colin Cowie Lifestyle, NYC; wedding consultant Corinne Strauss of Hampton.

Weddings, NY; Annie at Annie & Co. Silk Flowers, Vancouver; Nic Faitos at Starbright Floral Designs, NYC; Gerard Musella at Richard Salome Flowers Inc., NYC; Luis Collazo at Lotus Florists; Bobbi Hicks of Weddings by Bobbi, Sarasota, FL; and Gabriella at Ferrara Café, NYC.

Photography Credits

Front cover: Mallory Samson (top left), Toshi Otsuki (top right and bottom left), Starr Ockenga (bottom right)

Back cover: Mallory Samson

Page 2: Luciana Pampalone

Page 6: Jeff McNamara

Page 8: Mallory Samson

Page 9: Mallory Samson

Page 10: Toshi Otsuki

Page 12: Mallory Samson

Page 13: Mallory Samson

Page 14: Toshi Otsuki

Page 15: Toshi Otsuki

Page 16: Mallory Samson

Page 17 (upper): Jeff McNamara

Page 17 (lower): Jim Bastardo

Page 19: Mallory Samson

Page 20: Mallory Samson

Page 22: Luciana Pampalone

Page 24: Toshi Otsuki

Page 25: Mallory Samson

Page 26: Mallory Samson

Page 27: Mallory Samson

Page 28: Jim Bastardo

Page 29: Jim Bastardo

Page 30: Jim Bastardo

Page 31: Toshi Otsuki

Page 32: Toshi Otsuki

Page 35: Mallory Samson

Page 36: Mallory Samson

Page 37: Jim Bastardo

Page 38: Mallory Samson

Page 39: Toshi Otsuki

Page 42: Mallory Samson

Page 44: Mallory Samson

Page 45: Mallory Samson

Page 46: Toshi Otsuki

Page 47: Mallory Samson

Page 48: Mallory Samson

Page 49: Steven Randazzo

Page 51: Toshi Otsuki

Page 52: Mallory Samson

Page 54: Luciana Pampalone

Page 56 (upper): Mallory Samson

Page 56 (lower): William P. Steele

Page 57 (upper): Mallory Samson

Page 57 (lower): Mallory Samson

Page 58 (upper): Toshi Otsuki

Page 58 (lower): Jeff McNamara

Page 59: Toshi Otsuki

Page 60: Toshi Otsuki

Page 62: Jeff McNamara

Page 63: Jeff McNamara

Page 64: Toshi Otsuki

Page 66: Mallory Samson

Page 67: Mallory Samson

Page 68: William P. Steele

Page 69: Toshi Otsuki

Page 70: Mallory Samson

Page 71: Mallory Samson

Page 72: Mallory Samson

Page 74: Toshi Otsuki

Page 76: Toshi Otsuki

Pate 79: Toshi Otsuki

Page 80: Toshi Otsuki

Page 81: Jeff McNamara

Page 82: Toshi Otsuki

Page 85: Toshi Otsuki

Page 86: Toshi Otsuki

Page 88: Jeff McNamara

Page 90: Toshi Otsuki

Page 92: Toshi Otsuki

Page 94: David Prince

Page 96: Mallory Samson

Page 97: Mallory Samson

Page 98: Toshi Otsuki

Page 99: Toshi Otsuki

Page 100: Luciana Pampalone

Page 101: Christopher Drake

Page 102: Toshi Otsuki

Page 104: Toshi Otsuki

Page 105: Mallory Samson

Page 106: Toshi Otsuki

Page 108: Mallory Samson

Page 110: Toshi Otsuki

Page 112: Richard W. Brown

Page 118: David Prince

Page 121: Toshi Otsuki

Page 123: David Prince

Page 125: Wendi Schneider

Page 127: Starr Ockenga

Page 128: David Prince

Page 131 (left): Toshi Otsuki

Page 131 (right): Toshi Otsuki

Page 133: Luciana Pampalone

Page 134: Jana Taylor

Page 136 (Amaryllis): John Glover

Page 136 (Anemone): Toshi Otsuki

Page 136 (Aster): John Glover

Page 136 (Calla Lily): John Glover

Page 137 (Camellia): John Glover

Page 137 (Canterbury Bells):
John Glover

Page 137 (Chrysanthemum):
John Glover

Page 137 (Cosmos): John Glover

Page 137 (Cornflower): John Glover

Page 138 (Dutch Tulip: Minh + Wass

Page 139 (Daffodil): John Glover

Page 139 (Dahlia): Marina Schinz

Page 139 (Daisy): John Glover

Page 139 (Delphinium): John Glover

Page 139 (Forget-Me-Not):
John Glover

Page 139 (Freesia): John Glover

Page 139 (French Tulip):
Toshi Otsuki

Page 139 (Gardenia): John Glover

Page 140 (Gerbera Daisy):
John Glover

Page 140 (Gladiolus): John Glover

Page 140 (Grape Hyacinth):
John Glover

Page 140 (Hyacinth): John Glover

Page 140 (Hydrangea): Toshi Otsuki

Page 140 (Iris): John Glover

Page 140 (Lilac): John Glover

Page 140 (Lily): John Glover

Page 141 (Lily of the Valley):
David Prince

Page 142 (Orchid): John Glover

Page 142 (Peony): David Prince

Page 142 (Phlox): John Glover

Page 142 (Ranunculus):
Elizabeth Zeschin

Page 142 (Rose): Jennifer Jordan

Page 143 (Stephanotis): John Glover

Page 143 (Sunflower): John Glover

Page 143 (Sweet Pea): David Prince

Page 143 (Veronica): John Glover

Page 143 (Zinnia): John Glover

Page 144: Mallory Samson

Page 146: Luciana Pampalone

Page 147: Toshi Otsuki

Page 148: David Prince

Page 149: Wendi Schneider

Page 151: Mallory Samson

Page 152: William Meppem

Page 155: David Prince

Page 158: William Meppem

Page 160: Mallory Samson

Page 161 (upper): Toshi Otsuki

Page 161 (lower): Luciana Pampalone

Page 162 (upper): Toshi Otsuki

Page 162 (lower): Toshi Otsuki

Page 163: Wendi Schneider

Page 164 (left): Thomas Hooper

Page 164 (right): Thomas Hooper

Page 165: Mallory Samson

Page 166: Mallory Samson

Page 167 (left): Laura Resen

Page 167 (right): Jana Taylor

Page 168 (left): Toshi Otsuki

Page 168 (right): Jana Taylor

Page 170: Toshi Otsuki

Page 172: William Meppem

Page 174 (upper): Toshi Otsuki

Page 174 (lower): Toshi Otsuki

Page 175: Toshi Otsuki

Page 176 (upper): Toshi Otsuki

Page 176 (lower): Wendi Schneider

Page 177: Luciana Pampalone

Page 179 (upper): Toshi Otsuki

Page 179 (lower): Toshi Otsuki

Page 180: William Meppem

Page 181: David Prince

Page 182 (left): Mallory Samson

Page 182 (right): William Meppem

Page 183 (upper): Toshi Otsuki

Page 183 (lower): Toshi Otsuki

Page 184: Toshi Otsuki

Page 186: William Meppem

Page 187: William Meppem

Page 188 (left): William Meppem

Page 188 (right): William Meppem

Page 189: Toshi Otsuki

Page 190: Mallory Samson

Page 191: Courtesy of *Victoria*
Magazine

Page 193: Toshi Otsuki

Page 194: Mallory Samson

Page 195: Toshi Otsuki

Page 196 (left): William Meppem

Page 196 (right): Toshi Otsuki

Page 197: Mallory Samson

Page 198: David Montgomery

Page 199 (left): Toshi Otsuki

Page 199 (right): Toshi Otsuki

Page 200: Mallory Samson

Page 201: Toshi Otsuki

Page 202: Toshi Otsuki

Page 204: Toshi Otsuki

Page 207: Toshi Otsuki

Index